GOD DOES HAVE A SENSE OF HUMOR

Good luck,
God bless,
Keep Smiling!

Dec '20

GOD DOES HAVE A SENSE OF HUMOR

❀

Rob Ballister

iUniverse, Inc.
New York Lincoln Shanghai

GOD DOES HAVE A SENSE OF HUMOR

iUniverse books may be ordered through booksellers or by contacting:

iUniverse
2021 Pine Lake Road, Suite 100
Lincoln, NE 68512
www.iuniverse.com
1-800-Authors (1-800-288-4677)

Because of the dynamic nature of the Internet, any Web addresses or links contained in this book may have changed since publication and may no longer be valid.

The views expressed in this work are solely those of the author and do not necessarily reflect the views of the publisher, and the publisher hereby disclaims any responsibility for them.

ISBN: 978-0-595-36343-8 (pbk)
ISBN: 978-0-595-67368-1 (cloth)
ISBN: 978-0-595-80780-2 (ebk)

Printed in the United States of America

*To Mrs. Greer McKenna, who made me write before
I realized that I like to write.*

Contents

❀

It's funny, but I never set out to write a book. I began writing as a high school assignment, and continued because during my (successful) fight with cancer it was a way to exercise my mind when I couldn't exercise my body. So one thing led to another and eventually there were enough pages for a book, and here it is.

What follows is a collection of stories about things that I have seen or heard or experienced throughout my life, spanning over 20 years. They don't go in perfect chronological order, but there is a general progression through my life up to the present. The specific facts are not important, but the emotions, experiences, and especially the people are. These stories are not intended to educate or preach or offend or anything else but entertain. Some are almost completely fact, because it can be stranger than fiction. Some are absolutely fabricated. Most are somewhere in between. But I hope they all make you smile.

Special thanks to my super-supportive family and my wonderful wife Ivy for allowing me to pursue this dream.

Enjoy.

—RB

Cancer Hits, and I Hit Back

This was one of my earlier stories, and it was an attempt to help mentally heal after being diagnosed with cancer.

❧　　　❧　　　❧

Some time in my past, I remember hearing a debate on whether or not God had a sense of humor. I've never doubted that for a second. Ever look at a platypus? It looks like a drunken frat boy's biology experiment.

There is of course evidence from my own life as well. Not too long ago, I was diagnosed with cancer. That in itself is not funny. However, the corresponding events do get rather humorous, because I didn't have just any cancer. I had a type of cancer that was both relatively easily treated and cured, and at the same time, extremely embarrassing. I had testes cancer. As you can imagine, this was not something easily discussed, especially with the female of the species. Let me give you an example of how a conversation on the subject with a woman usually developed.

GIRL: Oh, you have cancer! That's terrible!

ME (in a manly, martyr-like tone): Why, yes, it is.

GIRL: You poor thing. Where do you have it?

ME (starting to look around the room): Uh, in my body.

GIRL: Oh, you poor dear! Where in your body?

ME (having a coughing spasm): (Cough, cough, cough)

GIRL: Excuse me?

ME (mumbling): moomphmeemphteiclmpmhd

- 1 -

GIRL: I'm sorry, it sounded like you said, "I need an icicle."

ME (wishing I was somewhere else, whispering): In my testicles.

GIRL: Oooooooooooohhhhhhhhhhhhhhhh.

That is usually when I fervently began to pray for death.

The truth is I may no longer have the cancer. For certain, I no longer have the testicle. One minute, I am checking into Naval Air Station Pensacola for flight training, and the next I am checking into the hospital to have renegade pieces of me removed. Do not pass go, do not collect $200, and do not eat for at least six hours before we go in and begin removing organs.

I was admitted into the hospital for what is medically referred to as a left orchiectomy. As far as I can tell, this title was to totally baffle everyone involved, including the patient. I refer to it as simply "my first operation," because to this point I have only had two and therefore know exactly which one I am talking about. Most people refer to it as neutering.

Though the doctor took great pains in explaining what was going to happen throughout the procedure, he lost me, and I had no idea what he was talking about. As near as I could tell, they were going to pinch my left ear to make me numb from my belly button down. Then they were going to slice open my foot, travel up my leg, do two laps around my heart, break for lunch, curse a little bit, remove my testicle with a handy pocket knife, and just for kicks, poke my liver. Following the operation, I would recover someplace called "I-See-You," which is misnamed, because I was asleep and couldn't see anyone.

While recovering from the operation, I was awakened every half hour so the hospital staff could say cheery things like, "And how are *we* feeling?" and congratulate me on urinating. My only thought was that they were all nuts, and I was missing one. After that they would all go in a back room and make one-testicle jokes until it was time to awaken me and poke or prod me with some blunt cold instrument.

I was released from the hospital only when I promised I wouldn't tell anyone how bad the food was (I used my pancakes to prop the window open). While I was recovering at home, the pathology on my now ownerless testicle came back. The tumor in my testicle was malignant. Actually, it was *very* malignant. Like kick puppies malignant; real bad news.

Now that I had cancer, it was time to see how much I had. In order to determine that, I had to have something called a CAT scan. I don't know the scientific particulars, but the basic idea is they put you in a room with a cat. If the cat likes you, you are fine. If not, you get sent back to the operating room. I have never met a cat I didn't try to kick, so you can tell what the outcome was.

Now comes the really funny part. It seems like this next surgery I needed, called "exploratory surgery" because the doctor had never done this before, had some serious side effects. Again, this was a complicated procedure. My understanding was that the doctor, while hopping up and down on one foot and singing the National Anthem, was going to remove my lymph nodes using a butter knife, a hacksaw, and some 10W-30 motor oil. While this sounded safe, there was a slight possibility that when I woke up, I might not be able to have kids. I would, however, not need any servicing for the next 3,000 miles.

To combat this side effect, it was necessary to go to a sperm bank in order to "put some away." This way, if my wife needed to be artificially inseminemi-namated, my kids would look like me instead of some college kid who needed $50 for beer. This process turned out to be *the* single most embarrassing event of my life. First of all, every person who worked in the clinic was female. Not only that, they were all attractive females, and they were all smirking, no doubt because this 22-year-old male just drove 90 minutes to work the self-service pump at life's gas station of love. That station turned out to be a small room with a leather recliner, a specimen cup, some "visual aides," and a sign:

The staff is to smile, answer the phones, and giggle while you are in here. They are not to lend a hand.

After escorting me to the room, the receptionist pleasantly said, "When you are finished, place your specimen here, and then skulk shamefully out that (she pointed) door."

It was very important to have "visual aides," because at the moment I was feeling about as romantic as a lethargic steer. The "visual aides" did prove to be uplifting, with the exception of the East German Playboy and the Middle East Swimsuit issue, and soon I was asking for a cigarette and pondering raiding the fridge.

This process was repeated three times in one week, after which the pretty blond lady behind the counter charged me three hundred dollars. This put a strain on our relationship, and I haven't called her since. My roommate reminded me when I got home that I could have probably gotten a hooker for less, and wouldn't have driven ninety minutes one way, either. He was very supportive.

And then it was time for the second surgery. For this, it was necessary for my intestines to be squeaky clean, so the doc gave me four liters of Roto-

Rooter to drink. That was an experience best left to your imagination, so I won't go into it.

I reported to the hospital at zero dark thirty in the morning, and was immediately dressed in a hospital gown and put in a bed. I wasn't tired or uncomfortable in my military uniform, but I later found out that this is standard procedure when checking into the hospital, in order to increase the general amount of humiliation felt by the patient. Urinating in a bottle is not enough.

They put me in the bed but wouldn't let me sleep, as every three or four minutes a different nurse would come in and ask me how I was feeling or some other equally pointless question. Feeling? *Feeling*?!? I was about to have major surgery which would keep me on my back for at least a week, with no solid food for three days (Mmmm, those IVs are good). I had already been poked and prodded several times and it wasn't even seven o'clock yet. I was feeling pretty damn miserable, thank you very much. This did not at all diminish the hospital staff's determination to keep asking me inane questions. Even when I threatened one of them with violence, she just smiled and kept right on being pleasant. I am never again entering a hospital without a concealed stun gun.

They wheeled me into the OR and gave me some drugs. Drugs are great. All of a sudden I was very mellow and nice to everyone. I even proposed to the OR tech. Unfortunately, he was a man, so this should give some indication of where my mind was. Then I fell asleep. The biggest medical event of my life, and I slept through the entire thing.

When I awoke six hours later, my first thought was, "I am not dead. Cool." Then the pain hit, and my next thought was, "Damn, I wish I was dead." My first words were, "Dad, I need a beer." Much of the first two days were spent slipping in and out of consciousness and alternating between asking for beer and hard liquor. When I was finally released from ICU, they put me in a chair and wheeled me down to the ward where I would continue to recover. The doc came in and pulled out the rest of my tubes. There were quite a few, and they *all* hurt very much coming out. He then told me, "I want you walking around today." I told him that I wanted him walking into a bus today. Get up? Maybe next year, doc. But I did it. I got up and walked four steps with only three orderlies holding up my limp body.

Despite the medical community's best efforts, I was released from the hospital six days later. I have a fourteen-inch scar running down my upper body, which I explain by telling people I was an extra in the movie *Aliens*. I am expected to recover fully. The hospital staff now calls me at home to ask me inane questions. The platypus is thriving. Tell me the Big Man does not have a sense of humor.

Church with God, the Hatfields, and the McCoys

One day in church, I actually sat behind the two families described below. It was the most entertaining time I have ever spent in church (well, except for my buddy's wedding, where he, the groom, passed out, but that's another story).

❧   ❧   ❧

Church: a place of peace, love, and harmony. Hopefully. It actually can depend on whom you are in church with. I'll explain. Last Sunday I sat behind two "partial" families. I'll define partial. On the left, we have the Hatfields. Mama Hatfield, little Karen Hatfield, cute as a button at three years, and Baby Hatfield, blabberingly oblivious to his surroundings at age 12 months. In the same pew, we have the McCoy family. Papa McCoy, Jon-boy McCoy, a very mature ten years, his brother Patrick "Hair Redder than a Carrot" McCoy (age eight) and their sister Elizabeth "Hair Redder than Patrick's" McCoy, tipping the scales at around two years.

Act One, Scene One. Lizzy McCoy is crawling all over Papa McCoy, Jon-boy McCoy, the pew, the kneeler, and the thirteenth station of the cross. Little Karen Hatfield is trying (vainly) to put Mama Hatfield's sunglasses on without a) poking herself in the eye; b) rearranging a nasal passage; or c) performing a do-it-yourself tracheotomy. Lizzy McCoy is talkative (she occasionally breaks out with a single word 17 consecutive times). Karen Hatfield is quiet.

Act One, Scene Two. Lizzy McCoy has succeeded in annoying her father enough for him to invoke that time-honored fatherly tradition of bottle-giving followed by eye-rolling followed by attempting to stuff the child in the mis-elette rack. Karen Hatfield has succeeded in putting Mama Hatfield's sunglasses on, albeit upside down. Now Lizzy McCoy begins to cry because she thinks Karen Hatfield is a giant fly. Karen seizes the opportunity, and steals Lizzy's bottle. The parents step in and separate the two, returning all possessions to their rightful owners, and vowing before God and the congregation never to even consider more children.

Act One, Scene Three. Baby Hatfield begins to cry. Loudly. For no reason. Mama Hatfield picks him up, talks baby-talk to him, and bounces him on her knee. Baby Hatfield responds by spitting up and crying louder. Lizzy McCoy shouts "baby" seven times before Papa McCoy gives her another bottle. Karen observes her fingers.

Intermission. Mama Hatfield takes Baby Hatfield to the bathroom to wash. While she is gone, Karen Hatfield re-acquaints herself with Lizzy McCoy by pulling her hair repeatedly.

Act Two, Scene One. Lizzy McCoy and Karen Hatfield, now longtime friends, exchange solemn gifts. Karen Hatfield gives Lizzy Mama Hatfield's keys. Lizzy McCoy reciprocates with (look out!) sunglasses. Karen Hatfield immediately puts them on (with help from Patrick McCoy, who I think is hitting on her), and they look more outlandish on her than her mother's did, even right side up. This sends me into hysterics, which is extremely painful because I have to hold it in. I am, after all, in church. The result is a vibrating butt massage for everyone in my pew, as I shake uncontrollably and am slapped on the arm by my female companion.

Act Two, Scene Two. The Finale. Baby Hatfield is crying again, probably because Lizzy McCoy is biting him. Karen Hatfield says nothing as she is pushed out of the way by Patrick McCoy, who is trying to stop his sister Lizzy. Lizzy breaks into a dead run after the offertory procession. Patrick, in hot pursuit, trips over his shoe laces and goes down hard. Mama Hatfield is trying to console her bitten child. Karen Hatfield, now virtually blind with her new shades, bumps into a pew, and succeeds in looking more dazed than before. Mama Hatfield attempts to remove the sunglasses and breaks them. Karen Hatfield cries. Mama Hatfield cries. The priest offers to perform an exorcism on Lizzy and Karen if they promise to leave now.

After Communion, the Hatfields and McCoys race to see who can clear the church first. The Hatfields win, only because the McCoys have to go back for Patrick, who still hasn't picked himself off of the floor.

I've always been sure of the existence of God, and last Sunday proved to me yet *again* that He indeed has a sense of humor.

Santa Claus, and Childhood Innocence Lost

This is one of those rare instances where I actually had a point to the story.

❈　　　❈　　　❈

If you could pick one moment in your life, one single event that marked the end of your childhood, what would it be? Looking back, what happened to you that made you take the childhood glasses off?

I have often thought about that. There are quite a few moments to choose from. I thought maybe it was when I graduated from college, but by then I already had a lot of the good and bad qualities of adulthood, so that wasn't it. Same with high school. I briefly thought that maybe it was the first time I kissed a girl, or held her hand, but then I realized that I was more confused about the mythical opposite sex after such events, and couldn't see how *that* was the turning point. No, something happened before those historic moments in my life. I pondered it for quite a while before I finally figured out what it was. Are you ready? It was Santa Claus, or rather his non-existence, that was the turning point for me.

I remember the day well, although I don't remember how old I was, maybe nine or ten. I was playing with my friend Bryan, and having a great time re-enacting World War II across my basement. Somehow, we got to talking about what we wanted for Christmas. My mom, doing the laundry in the next room, overheard us, and as I went on and on about what I was going to ask Santa for, I guess she thought it was time I learned the truth about St. Nick. So she told me.

I was stunned. Bryan, a much more seasoned veteran of childhood than I, already had heard, and was just being polite by not laughing out loud when I mentioned the jolly fat man in the red suit. All I could think of to say in my shock was, "I guess there is no Easter Bunny either?" More disappointment, this time accompanied by laughter from Bryan. I guess that was too much for him to take.

This was not an easy thing to handle. A basic tenet of my childhood was now smoldering wreckage. The holidays would always be there, but the mystery, the magic of it all, was gone. I quickly suppressed my emotions, as I could not let Bryan see my eyes begin to water. We were, after all, re-enacting WWII on my basement rug, and did Patton ever cry?

I don't mean to say that at that instant, *boom*, I was a man, ready to go out and get married and buy a car, quickly, before I turned eleven and was over the hill. But at that instant, a lot—not all, but a good amount—of the naiveté of childhood melted away. I no longer looked through the glasses of childhood. I actually took them off for the first time, and wow, did things look different.

I have had quite a few more disappointments in life since the Santa balloon burst. I have recovered from all of them (though financially the auto accident is still troublesome) and have learned a very important lesson. Just because someone removes the childhood glasses does *not* mean that you can't put them back on occasionally, and bark like a dog or watch the Muppet Show or whatever. Looking at life through the glasses of childhood is a way of dealing with stress. Sometimes I consider assault, but that can get costly.

The holidays are still there. And so is the magic. It's just in a different place. It is in the eyes of my little brother, and my neighbor's baby, and my little cousin, and when I put the glasses back on, it is in my eyes, too. Don't forget to put on your glasses every now and then. Sometimes, I *still* believe in Santa Claus.

There is Plenty of Crying in T-Ball

Growing up, I helped my father coach my brother's little league team for three years. We had a great time, and I met some great people, plus it was a chance for my dad and I to get closer, something we weren't able to do when I was really young because he worked a lot back then.

❧　　　❧　　　❧

They say that in order to experience everything in life, one must travel the globe in search of new experiences. I say baloney. You could travel the globe in search of new experiences, but if you are too cheap or hate foreign food, you could just coach Little League.

It's the midpoint of the season, and I have arrived at the conclusion that when it's over I will either be ready for anything life throws at me or dead from a stomach ulcer. In only eight brief games, I have seen so many unbelievable things that any doubts about the existence of God or His sense of humor are long gone. I have seen sure home-runs turn into outs because the other team's center fielder was really Roberto Clemente reincarnate. I have seen sure outs turn into home-runs because my center-fielder was mesmerized by a lady bug on his shoelace. There have been games with scores that sound like basketball games, and games that were tied at zero going into the following Tuesday.

Keep in mind that the team is made up of 16 future stars, between the ages of six and eight years old. All of them have runny noses. Not one of them has a glove smaller than his upper body or pants that fit. They all bat with bats at least six inches taller and several pounds heavier than they are. At least two of them are comatose since birth, and one of them is possessed. Some of them have played before, and some of them *still* haven't seen a baseball. They keep their eyes shut, for fear of actually being productive.

The "veterans," if that term can be applied to seven-and eight-year-olds, can throw, catch, hit, and run bases. The new children, or "monkeys," can duck, trip, sniffle, fall down, strike out, and cry. They also have a tendency to get lost between first and second base and wander aimlessly about right field until I rescue them. In all fairness, though, they are trying (very).

The other coaches and I have been lucky in that the parents of our players, as a group, are all very supportive, and we have the biggest cheering section of any team in our league. Coincidentally, we also have the highest average alcohol consumption. However, you can't please everyone all the time, and there are those times when we are asked, "Why doesn't my son/daughter/clueless-lump play more?" from a disgruntled parent. To that question the response is, "Because he's not warmed up yet" or, "We're rotating." The real truth is the child would either get lost at his position or run in terror from a slow grounder, but few parents want to hear such things.

Being a T-ball coach requires patience, politics, not a little bit of luck, and a strong sedative. This is my second season and I think that I'm finally getting the hang of it. Despite the bobbles, overthrows, underthrows, and general chaos, we have managed to compile an eight wins, no losses record, and are on our way to our second winning season. Whether it's because we're good, or we're lucky, or because the rest of the coaches are worse off than we are I don't know, but if T-ball is anything like life, (scary thought) than it's a little bit of each.

Flight of the Rolling Coffin

This is what too much time plus unlimited access to power tools does to young engineer wannabees. Parents, learn from this.

❧   ❧   ❧

Did you ever build a go-cart as a kid? My buddies and I did. Several, actually. Each was faster, more stylish, and of course, in the cool-guy fashion, more dangerous than the last. Kind of like the women I have dated.

My first attempt was pretty basic, which was fitting, because we were eight years old, and also pretty basic. We dragged my old red wagon to the top of the hill. I sat in it, flipped the handle up, and off we went. To make it more car-like, I eventually covered it with a piece of cardboard and cut a hole in which I could sit. Major improvements, in my eyes. It still didn't have seatbelts, brakes, roll bars, cigarette lighter, or any of the other thousand safety features one's mother would hope for in a do-it-yourself go-cart. It was a start, however.

Our next attempt involved nailing several pieces of lumber together and attaching lawnmower wheels. I was head design engineer on this project, and took my work very seriously. I made several drawings, which looked very official on the green graph paper that I used. I actually paid more attention to the green graph paper than to such trivial details as a steering system and brakes.

I would like to digress for a moment and point out something of great significance to all the budding engineers in the audience. Green graph paper *always* makes things look more official. I pointed this out several years later when one of my college professors obviously gave me the wrong grade. "But I used green graph paper," I pointed out.

"Yes, you did," he replied, "but this is an English class."

If you ever come to a point where you are totally lost—I did, it was called "junior year"—just present some numbers and a few scribbles on some green graph paper and you are virtually guaranteed to make an impression on your professor. Please note that I did not say "virtually guaranteed to graduate".

Anyway, there was some disconnect between me and the head production engineer/mechanic/snack-and-soda guy. He almost built it the way I drew it, and the wheels and axles almost stayed on the way he built it, and his little brother almost didn't get hurt when he drove it. Our design firm/friendship dissolved shortly thereafter. On the bright side, so did his brother's internal stitches.

Two years later, another buddy whom I had yet to injure and I decided that there was not enough danger in our lives and began to build the ultimate go-cart. Something that would be eternal. Something that would last long after we were gone, or at least back in school.

We began to prepare. I stockpiled green graph paper and pencils. We inventoried my garage. My dad said we could use "some" of the plywood sheets there. I think my definition of "some" was slightly more generous than his. His was very near to "three," and mine was slightly closer to "all." My buddy "obtained" wheels from his neighborhood. Never mind what his definition of "obtained" was.

We began the design. We figured out how tall we would be when we were in college, how big our feet would grow, and how long our legs would be. We wanted this thing to fit us like a glove when we were eighty years old and tooth-less. We never really discussed why two toothless eighty-year-old men would want to be riding around in a go-cart. These were important design consider-ations. Again, brakes and steering fell by the wayside.

For weeks, my garage was a virtual flurry of sawdust and plywood scraps. We drilled. We cut. We sanded. And behold, when we finished, we had created the ultimate soapbox masterpiece—the rolling coffin.

It was big. It was heavy; we put an anvil in the front for extra momentum. It had "Get out of our way or we'll ruin your day!" emblazoned in bright green letters on it. Black would have been better, but we had just painted the lawn, and had to work with the materials on hand. It possessed the deadly elegance that one would expect of an ultra-lethal fighter aircraft, or perhaps a super galactic space fighter. At least we thought so until the glue fumes wore off. In reality, it was a big box on wheels, but we didn't have much to get excited about back then.

It was time for our first road test. We stole his older brother's moped helmet (not for protection, but to look cool) and dragged, pushed, and pulled our creation to top of the adjoining dead-end street, which happened to be on a hill. His older brother stood guard at the bottom of the hill, watching for cars. We drew straws, and he pulled the short one, so I got to ride first. At this point, we were still incredibly confident in our design. We would learn.

As my friend gave the coffin a push, I remember the joy and exhilaration of the wind on my face as the adrenaline flowed through my veins. I remember the sun, and the smells, and then I remember my buddy's older brother began waving and saying something about a car …

And that is the last thing I remember. But I will fill you in on the details, as I read them from the police report.

I apparently went hurdling through the intersection, which 99% of the time has exactly zero cars in it. At this particular moment, it had exactly four. One was heading away from me, and one was stopped at a stop sign, so that left two. With horns blaring and fists shaking, the drivers swerved to miss what to them looked like a storage crate with an alien sitting in it that had suddenly appeared in the middle of the street. Because I had no idea what "load tests" were, amidst the screeching, cursing, and general chaos of that first ride, one of my tires literally disintegrated. This sent me careening out of control into a neighbor's swimming pool, via their back porch. One of the cars ended up in a living room via a bay window, so I did not complain.

Our driving days were over. I was grounded. My buddy is *still* grounded (his parents were always pretty strict). I no longer aspire to build go-carts, as I still have many painful memories of the incident, along with some pretty cool scars. I am, however, 35% done with the design on my homemade airplane. As soon as my buddy is allowed out, we plan to get started.

Death by Spanish

My Spanish teacher drove me absolutely crazy, but it's funny to look back on it now.

❦   ❦   ❦

The experts say that high school is the best four years of a person's life. I would very much like to agree with them, but unfortunately I can't. Everyday I have to go to school, and my first class every day is Spanish, and if Spanish class is part of the best four years of my life, I'm going to jump off the Brooklyn Bridge now before things get any worse.

Perhaps I can put this in better perspective. I'm not Spanish. I never was Spanish. I never will be Spanish. I never even want to be Spanish, so why do I have to knock myself out to learn the language? Just recently I figured out that in English the adjective almost always goes before the noun modified, and now some teacher with an accent I can't understand no matter what language she speaks keeps telling me that in Spanish the adjective almost always goes after the noun modified. I am a peaceful person, but much more of this could make me *loco*.

This would be easier to understand if you realized what goes on every morning in a typical Spanish class. Please try to follow along, I know it gets horrible, but remember, I live this.

The teacher walks in every morning in an outfit so outlandish that naturally half the class keels over laughing (not me, of course). Instead of ignoring it, the teacher always asks some poor slob (that *would* be me) why half the class is in tears on the floor. Because I can't be honest and say, "Because you shot your couch and dressed in the carcass," I just sit there and grin sheepishly. Already,

I'm in Hell, and class just started. Ten minutes later everybody is back in their seats and we are ready to begin.

Every morning, the teacher addresses the class, not with "Good morning, class," or even "Hola, classe," which we would understand, but with "Buenomananacubanahavanapinadapinacoladahablaba." What does this mean? I don't have the faintest idea, so I just nod my head and repeat "Si," over and over. I know someone in the class must understand, but that person is afraid to speak up for fear of being stoned to death by the rest of us uneducated heathens. Then the teacher says, in unrecognizable English, "Open your work-books to page five hundred eighteen." Because there are only one hundred ten pages in our workbooks, we know she means fifty eight. When we arrive at the day's lesson, the teacher gives us our assignment. "OK, do essersisses ah, beh, se, de, eh, an effe, an no talking!" I look at the assignment, and I notice that the first exercise has thirty parts, each with three sub-parts. I go to read the directions, and they are in Spanish. It is at this point every day that I turn to my friend and say, "You distract her, I'll beat her to death with the Spanish flag," or words to that effect.

I'd continue, but because there are respectable, decent people reading this, my morals prevent me. I am all for exposure to foreign culture and language, but wouldn't it be easier just to watch movies or something?

Sex Education as Taught by Nuns

Among my friends, this tale is one of the more popular. This was my attempt to put into words one of the truly most awkward periods of my life. Maybe of anyone's life.

❈　　　　❈　　　　❈

Freshman year in high school can be an exciting time of growth and development. The operative word is "can." It can also be, as in my case, a time of never ending awkwardness and embarrassment. I had acne. Girls would talk to me only long enough to turn me down for something. "No, I won't go to the movies with you." "No, I won't dance with you." "No, I will not loan you a pencil." "No I will not stop stepping on your neck." God, in his infinite wisdom, and to prove once more in my life that He does have a sense of humor, decided that now was the time to inspire the principal to inject Sexual Education into the curriculum.

One could argue that learning about sex in a classroom was a stimulating change from algebra and Shakespeare. One could also argue that because I wasn't learning anything "on the job," so to speak, it wouldn't be a bad idea to somehow prepare for that day so far in the future when some obviously misguided and desperate female would for some reason known only to God find me attractive. I personally made the argument that it was silly to teach someone how to cook if there was no way in Hell he was getting near the food, but the system rolled right over me (again).

I went to a Catholic high school, and sex education was placed into the lap of the religion department. Logic would dictate that it should probably be put into the hands of the Physical Education program, except in my school, having the coaches lecture about reproduction might encourage some of them to try it themselves. Believe me; no one in town wanted *that*. Besides, the Physical Education department already had responsibility for Driver's Education, and that was more than enough for their eight bodies and six brains to handle. But I digress.

Because the Religion department was responsible for Sexual Education, my teacher for that much-anticipated class turned out to be a nun. This made about as much sense as having a vegetarian teach a meat-cutting class. Nuns just aren't the type one opens up to with sexual questions, though better Sister than one of the Phys Ed Neanderthals. Sister could at least use complete sentences.

We had these little books with all kinds of words that one would never consider saying when a nun was around, so participation was minimal. This did not sit well with the school, so students were getting notes sent home saying, "Little Ronny won't participate in class discussions concerning the 's' word, certain 'm' words, and the female reproductive system. He also refuses to discuss his sexual feelings in front of 32 of his peers, both male and female. Is he gay?" This was McCarthy-ism for sure, though on a much smaller scale. The lack of participation led Sister to do much of the reading and discussing herself. Now *she* was using all those words we would never say around a nun, which was like hearing a lecture on racial tolerance from Adolf Hitler.

In addition, our books had several helpful diagrams, all in purple ink. I am not sure, but I doubt the female reproductive organs are purple, and I *know* (I just checked) mine aren't. What gives? I could just see my class mates on their honeymoons, "Honey, I am a little confused. Can we paint you purple?"

We also learned about birth control. That was actually sort of interesting. I always thought the barrier method was when she slammed the door in your face. Never mind what my definition of the rhythm method was.

I don't remember what I got in the class. I do know it went nowhere in teaching me to deal with the opposite sex, so now I am flailing around with so many other hapless males, and there does appear to be quite a lot of us. I will say that I am much more open around nuns, and that if I ever meet a purple woman, I will indeed be very well prepared.

Bachelor Life
(How to Clean a Bathroom with
a Flame-Thrower)

During my early career, I lived with one of my college buddies in Pensacola, FL. We were probably two of the most non-bachelors you could meet. We cleaned regularly, had decent furniture, and cooked things that didn't start off as frozen food. My Mom still would constantly rib me about the "bachelor life" that I was really only living in her mind. But the reality was pretty boring, so I wrote a story that was much closer to Mom's version.

❉   ❉   ❉

People often put down the bachelor lifestyle. I think that is because they really don't understand it. I live with a buddy from college in a totally female-less apartment, and to my mother's surprise, it is not a disorganized foul-smelling-poorly-decorated-overflowing-with-laundry-only-beer-and-leftover-burritos-in-the-fridge-when-will-you-clean-this-place-up cesspool. Back off, Mom, we don't even *eat* burritos.

Bachelors have a different outlook on life than normal people. For instance, bachelors have more than just "clean" and "dirty" laundry. There are several different levels in between. My own rule is you can't wear a shirt three days running without at the very least airing it out for a good half hour. My roommate has a similar rule concerning socks.

Bachelors don't cook. We create. There is absolutely no reason why you cannot have a peanut butter, potato, and tuna fish casserole, especially if there is nothing else in the pantry, or better yet the items were all on sale at the grocery store.

When it comes to groceries, if it is on sale, we are going to buy it. No questions, no arguments. We have three pounds of swordfish, seven boxes of au gratin potatoes, two five-pound bags of corn meal, and 16 cans of cat food. We haven't got the foggiest idea what to do with any of this stuff, as we don't even own a cat, but we did get a damn good deal on it. We accidentally picked up a sweet little old lady who got too close to a "Clearance Item" sign, but she threatened to sue before we got to the checkout, so we dropped her in the frozen foods case.

Despite popular belief, bachelors do own cleaning supplies. We have Windex and half a rag, and we clean religiously once a month whether the apartment needs it or not. I even tried to clean out the fridge once. I got as far as opening the door and looking inside. Then something that used to be meatloaf spoke up. "Just what do you think *you're* doing, fat boy? We don't knock on your bedroom door, do we? Beat it!" Then the cauliflower growled at me. I backed away and closed the door quietly. We have eaten out a lot since then.

My roommate handles cleaning the bathroom. He goes in once a month with a can of Lysol and a cigarette lighter. He proceeds to do a Rambo-with-flame-thrower impersonation on all surfaces and fixtures. Once that is done, he brings a garden hose through the window and rinses everything off. Crude, but very effective. We use a similar technique on pots and pans which are too big to fit into the dishwasher.

My own personal opinion is that God would not have created frozen food if he did not intend for bachelors to exist somewhere on the evolution ladder. Yeah, it might be one of the lower rungs, but when it's ten o'clock in the morning, and I'm dressed in a beer and my Kermit the Frog boxer shorts, I don't care.

Blind Date Disasters

This story is a little out of order, and it doesn't really "fit" anywhere, but it is almost entirely true, so that's something.

❧   ❧   ❧

Friends are a wonderful gift. They are a rare and precious gift. There is a special bond among friends; one that transcends personal desires and well being. For those few that I consider a friend, I would honestly do anything.

I can say this with ease, because there are several things that I know my friends will never ask me to do. My friends will never ask to borrow my car, as it gets two gallons to the mile, doesn't go faster than 35 miles per hour, and only has three tires. My friends will never ask me to stay in my apartment, because we haven't found the last guy who tried. Finally, my friends will never, ever, under any circumstances, even if I pay them, ask me to set them up on a blind date.

I am actually pretty comfortable with this arrangement. I don't want people borrowing my car, *I* don't even stay in my own apartment, and I have had it with blind dates, either setting them up or being set up. I have yet to have a blind date that went better than the *Titanic*'s maiden voyage, and the ones I have set up for friends have been worse.

Because this would be really short if I didn't, I will give you a few choice examples to illustrate how bad I am at the whole blind date thing.

When I was in college, one of my friends knew this *great* girl who really wanted to go to one of our school dances. Being a kind, considerate gentleman, and also desperate, I agreed to meet with her. Fully expecting to meet a cross between Godzilla and Buffy the juggling female gorilla, I was pleasantly surprised when she turned out to be one *very* attractive young lady, complete with a pretty smile, a personality, and, I was happy to notice, breasts.

We appeared to hit it off great, and I couldn't wait to go to the dance with her. All was right with the world. And here comes the other shoe. She had a friend, and she wanted me to set her up with one of my friends, so we could all double date and go together. No problem, I thought. Great looking pseudo-goddesses always travel in groups, so her friend couldn't be *that* bad, could she?

OK, now many of you are expecting me to launch into a tirade on how ugly this friend turned out to be. Well, I can't do that, because she turned out to be almost as good looking as my date. Unfortunately, I also can't say that the evening went well. The two lovely young ladies decided that for whatever reason they would spend virtually the entire evening in the ladies room smoking. They came out only to check if we were still there and see if food was served. Then back to Camel-ot. In a four hour evening we saw them for about twenty-three minutes. My buddy and I dressed up in tuxedos, complete with ill-fitting shoes, in order to hang outside the ladies bathroom all evening. I don't even think we saw the dance floor. We did, however, almost get beat up by the female rugby team.

Finally, about ten minutes before the last song was to be played, here come the ladies, still gorgeous but reeking of smoke only slightly less than the Marlboro Man. My friend's date stated that she was bored, and asked if we would be interested in going back to her place to smoke some marijuana. Ignoring us all night in front of our friends wasn't enough; now they wanted to introduce us to the town Vice Squad. We didn't even drive them home.

OK, pretty bad for a blind date, but not catastrophic. Not enough to keep me from trying again, anyway.

Next chapter. I met an absolutely gorgeous girl at a mixer, whom I really wanted to see again. For the uneducated, a mixer is an informal dance where the turn out is about one girl for every seven guys. When you eliminate the ones that are too young to be there, too old to be there, or are just uglier than the south end of a mule, the ratio is more like 1:47. Because I had already staked out the ladies room at the last dance, I knew where to look and was able to hunt down one of the few women there who both needed a bra and knew what a toothbrush was for. I invited her down for our next formal dance, and, of course, she wanted to bring not one, but *two* friends. Quick to learn from the last fiasco, I demanded physical descriptions. She provided them quickly and efficiently, taking only the time necessary to lie.

Hearing her somewhat exaggerated descriptions (faces of angels, legs of goddesses, chests like small mountain regions), I immediately sought out my friend from "that smoking incident" described above in order to make restitution. Sadly, he isn't any brighter than me, and agreed to attend, and together we convinced a third unsuspecting party that I couldn't screw up *that* bad twice in a row. Everything was set, and we looked forward to the weekend with cheer in our hearts and condoms in our pockets.

When we arrived at the designated meeting place the afternoon of the dance, I immediately began scanning the room, praying against all hope that my new-found friend had heard of the rule about pseudo-goddesses traveling in packs. As my lovely companion stood up, my close friends' reactions shattered all my hopes. One of them, the survivor from "that smoking incident," said, "That better not be them." Contestant number two just sobbed and fell down.

I grabbed my one friend before he could get away. Together we picked the other guy off the floor and moved forward. We were, after all, gentlemen, and we could not disappoint these ladies. We also were in too much shock to think of legitimate excuses on why we suddenly had to leave.

Together, actually, the two friends weren't bad. Together, they averaged about 130 pounds, because one was 230 pounds and the other was about 35. Together, they had a full set of teeth, and together they wore enough makeup to adequately cover two people, though all of it was on the skinny one.

By the shrewd plan of offering anything of value I ever was to own to my two friends, I convinced them to proceed with the evening. We proceeded to a local restaurant, where the one debutante ate four plates of chicken, two pizzas, a cheeseburger deluxe combo, and a diet coke. The other had a half slice of bread. We paid the bill and left, but the girls caught up to us.

We drove them to the hotel so they could get ready for the dance. Just as I thought it couldn't get any worse, Ultra-behemoth turned to my one friend, the one whom I had screwed over with the last blind date disaster, and asked "How do you feel about feathers?" He just smiled, and the ladies got out of the car. He then turned to me and said, "She comes out looking like Big Bird, and God Himself won't be able to save you." This pretty much set the tone for the entire evening.

When we picked up the ladies for the dance, first my date came out, very attractive in her blue sequined evening dress. Following her came Miss Skinny dressed in something that made her disappear when she turned sideways. Finally, out came Feathers.

In her defense, she didn't look like Big Bird. That might have been an improvement, though. Her dress was this black sequined *thing* with black feathers all around the top. That wasn't so bad, but the feathered boa and the peacock feather hat were just too much. She was 5'8" without the hat. With it, she was slightly taller, something like 8'4". My two friends reacted to the appearance of their dates in two completely different ways. One went into convulsions; the other entered this trancelike state, bordering pretty much on a coma.

You would think that at this point there was no where for the evening to go but up. Well, the only thing that went up was my blood pressure. Here I was, trying to really impress my date with my gentlemanly qualities, and my buddies were doing everything they could to make the girls want to leave early. I put up with most of it, but when my one friend tried to light his date on fire, I thought that was a little much. Of course, my date didn't see my buddy try to roast her friend. All she saw was me stand up and throw water on Featherwoman for no apparent reason. That was not as easy to explain as one might think. Not that I got a chance, as both Featherwoman and my date came after me with the table centerpiece and some cookies, which at my school were *lethal*. The evening eventually ended with the town riot police being called out. Any bets on whether or not I got a second date?

There was a tradition in my school that at the end of each weekend, the freshmen would award a brick to the upperclassman who was seen with the most "aesthetically challenged" young lady. Following this particular weekend, the freshmen *built a cinderblock wall* in front of the room where Featherwoman's escort lived.

It took us three days to chisel him out. When he emerged, we all made a pact. That pact legally banned me from setting up any blind dates until the year 2006, and also stated that I was pretty much in debt to both my friends from that evening until approximately thirty seconds after I die.

Whenever we get together, we repeat this story, and everyone has a good laugh, except those of us that were actually involved. As far as my lovely lady, I haven't seen her since, and there is a restraining order keeping me from coming within three states of her. If you know someone that you want to introduce me to, do me a favor. Keep her.

Dating, Boxing, and the Eerie Similarities Between the Two

I have never been all that successful with the females of our great species. This story was an attempt to put some of that frustration into words, and maybe vent a bit. It didn't really work, but that's my problem. We were watching a boxing match at the time, but there's limited truth to the rest.

❋　　　　❋　　　　❋

My roommate and I were watching a boxing match on HBO the other night. My first thought, as I watched Poor Joe Schmoe get pummeled into the ring post by Steroid Man, was, "Better him than me." My second thought was, "This reminds me an awful lot of dating." I told this to my roommate. He asked me if I had been drinking. When I told him no, he said I should start immediately.

Actually, my social life is a lot like a really bad boxing match. The part of the heavyweight champ is played by the females. The part of the non-ranked, over-weight, trying-to-make-a-comeback-despite-being-horribly-underskilled challenger is played by yours truly. In the beginning, there are two people looking for an advantage over the other. There is some dancing. Words are exchanged. There are brief clenches, broken up by a third party; the referee or her mother—they usually look alike. There is sweat, and then the whole thing comes to a vicious violent end with me bleeding on the floor. The similarities are uncanny. The only obvious difference is that in a boxing match the loser doesn't pay for dinner.

OK, I am a little bitter. No, I am a *lot* bitter. But I have good reason. If there was a category titled, "Most Consecutive Worst Dates," Guinness would have beaten my door down years ago. I have been on some real winners, let me tell you. Observe as I step into the ring.

Well, Phil, the challenger looks fresh enough. Let's see how he does in the first round.

Round one was Tiffany. I took her to dinner at a quaint little dinner theater, where I learned that Tiffany hadn't been schooled in the finer arts of using silverware, or a napkin, or a drinking glass for that matter. More people were watching her strap on the feed bag (just about literally) than were watching the show. This caused the director to have me bodily removed from the theater by my ears. Tiffany is still there, as far as I know.

He's showing a little blood, Bob, but he still looks fresh in his corner.

Rebecca asked if it bothered me that she still lived with her parents. I said no, of course not. However, when I arrived to pick her up, her father was cleaning what appeared to be an automatic weapon on the front porch. I was a little uneasy, but not yet "bothered." Not to worry, it would get worse. As I introduced myself, he offered to show me around until Becky was ready. I accepted out of politeness (and fear; I think I saw him chamber a round in that thing). His basement would have reminded me of a gun shop, except a gun shop doesn't usually have so many explosives. Now I was "bothered." Becky and I left at seven thirty. I had her home by nine. Dad was planting land mines along the front walk. "You can't be too careful," he told me with a smile.

Tough round, Phil, but not much damage done. The kid still has some fight in him .

Ding, ding! Next into the ring was Sharon. After our date she invited me up to her apartment. She said she wanted to, "slip into something more comfortable so we could get, you know, a little physical." My juices were flowing. I thought, "Oh boy, am I going to see stars tonight!" How prophetic. Sharon returned in a white judo *gi*, which was held up by a black belt. Her "getting physical" involved wiping the floor with any part of my anatomy she could get a hold of. "Ooh, we just learned this last week. Let me show you." *Wham*!

I don't know. That was a rough beating. It could hurt him in the following rounds, Bob.

Angela thought she could cure world hunger by sending all the hungry people Happy Meals. Sandy said she wanted to be a vegetarian because she loved animals. Her best friend Monica only had a salad when we went to dinner. Why? "I'm a strict veterinarian," she said.

He's on the ropes, Phil! I think he is in trouble!

Veronica told me that she wasn't sure if she was a lesbian. About ten minutes later, I guess she figured it out because she disappeared with our waitress.

Kim was a Sagittarius, and demanded to be driven home when she found out I was a Libra. "Let's be realistic. We just aren't compatible. Your moon is ascending, and my stars are descending," she said. Yeah, well your marbles are missing, too.

It doesn't look good, Bob. He's on his feet, but does he know where he is?

Cindy's life ambition was to milk a cow. Understandable, considering they have about the same IQ.

Big trouble here, Phil. I think he's going down. He can't take much more …

Roxanne and I had a great time. She said that I wasn't superficial, that I was caring and understanding. She said that she felt like she could tell me anything. Then she told me she used to be a man. Caring and understanding be damned, she (he?) certainly could *not* tell me that!

OOHH! He's down. He's out. The ref could count to 100. Stick a fork in him, Bob, he's done!

I could go on, but the image of me bruised and bloody on the canvas pretty much sums it up. I'm not asking for the perfect date, but one that doesn't leave any scars would be nice. With my luck, God is a woman, and when I die I will continue to get pummeled until eternity.

My Mother the Great Film Director

This is one of those where pretty much every word is true. I'm a lot better at cherishing these moments now.

❁   ❁   ❁

It was Christmas, 1993 (some time after I had gotten over the Santa Claus thing). My grandparents gave a camcorder to my family. State of the art, too. All the bells and whistles and even a little remote control that fits into the side of the unit. Very high tech stuff.

My job was to read the instruction manual, which was almost as big as the New Testament, albeit with bigger type, and then teach the rest of the family how to use it. After much reading and button pushing, producing little whirrs and clicking noises, I was able to triumphantly take a motion picture of first my foot and then my family room ceiling, although I was aiming at neither.

Eventually, I smoothed out my technique and took some pretty good home movies of family Christmas-type activities, and began teaching my mother how to operate our little technological friend.

In doing so, I created a monster. My sweet, dear old mother was transformed into Francis Ford Coppola. The camera was everywhere, always, with my mother gleefully narrating to preserve for all of history the events of the Ballister household as they occurred. I grew rather annoyed, and often would stop what I was doing when the camera panned to me. This refusal was usually documented into the film just to spite me. It just seemed that with all the posing and camera action, with everyone trying to preserve and record the momentous occasion for future viewing, no one was enjoying the momentous occasion as it occurred in the present. "I can't wait to watch the tape. I was so busy filming it, I missed what actually happened," was what I imagined my mother saying.

Many years later, while rummaging around an old drawer, I found a picture of my sixth grade basketball team, which had been taken by one of our coaches. I knew I probably griped and complained about being in the picture, but looking back on it now, it was a treasure. It was a period of my life I had nearly forgotten; sixth grade was not my best school year, plus I had acne. It took me *ten years* to appreciate that one picture for what it was worth. Of course I couldn't appreciate the video Mom was shooting; my own memory was still as clear as the tape. Someday I will need those tapes to flesh out my memories and remind me of moments and family in the past, and while I may be too dense to realize this, Mom has picked up the ball for me.

Though none of this really makes me tolerate the camera any better, I realize that Mom's motives go beyond winning American Home Video contests or inconveniencing me for fun. She is appreciating and taking care of the memories until I realize the need to. So instead of being sarcastic or rolling my eyes when the camera comes out, I think next time I will just shut up and say, "Thanks Mom."

Little Children Making Big Noises

Another one of the roommate stories involving my friend Dave ...

✤ ✤ ✤

It seems that at least once a week you can read an article about noise. Usually, it concerns people complaining because they think the areas where they live are too noisy. They live near an airport or a highway or train tracks or some such thing that makes their lives difficult. Well, tough. I have them all beat, because I live with possibly the noisiest creatures on Earth; toddlers.

My roommate and I live behind Ms. Martin's Nursery School and Day Care Center, a.k.a. "the Zoo." Whatever we did in previous lives to deserve this, I assure you we are both *very* sorry, because apparently all these children are going to grow up to be fire alarms and police sirens. I can't believe the lungs on these kids. Monday thru Friday, eight a.m. to six p.m., there is constant screaming. We can hear nothing else. *Nothing* else. No polite toddler conversation about Bugs Bunny or Power Rangers. No games of Dodge Ball or Duck Duck Goose or any of that. Sometimes there is crying too, when one of the little monsters runs over another slightly slower little monster with the Big Wheel, so I guess it isn't truthful to say that *all* they do is scream. Entertaining as this is, it does not alleviate the noise problem.

Typical morning conversation during these hours in my apartment goes like this. Keep in mind that my roommate is sitting approximately three feet away from me.

ME (conversationally): Hey, Dave?

No answer.

ME (a little louder): Dave?

Still no answer.

ME (at the top of my lungs): *Daaaaaaaaavvvee!*

DAVE (at the top of his lungs): *Whhhhaaaaaaattttt?*

ME (still at the top of my lungs, accompanied by much gesturing): *Pass the butter, please!*

DAVE: *Sure!*

He immediately passes me the orange juice.

This can get extremely annoying after about twenty minutes, so I actually went to see Ms. Martin about her little bundles of terror. On the way to her office, I got a good look at what really goes on behind that woefully inadequate fence that separates my apartment complex from Ms. Martin's zoo. As I walked across the playground, there was this little kid, a boy about four, head back, eyes closed, just screaming at the top of his not so little lungs, for absolutely no reason. One of his buddies, whom I assumed was his relief, was looking on. When the first one stopped to catch his breath, the observer started. It was amazing. It was like the changing of the guard.

FIRST CHILD: *Aaaaaaaaaaaaaaaaaaaaaaaaa!* Oh, Bob, you're here. I didn't see you. Right on time though. Nothing new to report. Have a good watch.

SECOND CHILD: Thanks, Joe. Damn fine job you were doing. Go get yourself a cold milk. You've earned it.

FIRST CHILD: Thanks. See you at nap time.

SECOND CHILD: Right. *Aaaaaaaaaaaaaaaaaaaaaaaaaaaa!*

What on earth are they screaming about? I saw fifty-six screaming children, and not one of them had a reason to make noise (except the two I accidentally stepped on). No broken bones, no muggings, no-fall-down-go-boom, *nothing!* They were screaming for the pure, malicious joy of keeping everyone in my building on the verge of insanity.

I finally got in to see Ms. Martin. She was a sweet, gray haired, grandmotherly type. Apparently, her job was fairly hard on the body, as she was only 28 years old. Our conversation went like this.

ME (conversationally): Good morning, Ms. Martin.

MS. MARTIN: What's that, Deary?

ME (louder): I said, *good morning, Ms. Martin.*

MS. MARTIN (checking her watch): Ten thirty, dear.

ME (getting frustrated): *Ma'am, your kids are too loud!*

MS. MARTIN: Why, I'd love some coffee, thank you, Sonny!

ME (exasperated): *Goodbye, Ms. Martin.*

MS. MARTIN (cheerfully): Last door on the left. Don't forget to flush.

We have adjusted, my roommate and I. We wear earplugs whenever we are in the apartment, and have taken up sign language in order to communicate. The other day Ms. Martin came over to ask me to turn down my stereo. I gave her directions to the QwikMart. Let's see how she likes it.

Laundry, my Girlfriend, and the Destiny of my Wardrobe

I've mentioned that my success with women has been less than stellar, but there were too many in the world for me to avoid a girlfriend forever. What follows is the first of the "girlfriend" stories, though in the interest of self-preservation I never actually mention her name.

❀   ❀   ❀

Part of being a bachelor is learning to do your own laundry. I had been really spoiled all through my early life concerning laundry. Up until I went to college, I put my clothes in the hamper and *poof* they came back clean. College was just as good. Because I went to a military academy, I just put my laundry out in the hall every Tuesday, and *poof* it was back clean and pressed by Friday. The system worked and I did not want to upset the apple cart. Throughout my entire life the laundry fairies had taken care of it all, and that was fine with me.

Upon graduation, I received a rude awakening. The first week in my new apartment, I put my laundry out in the hall on Tuesday night, business as usual. Wednesday morning it was gone, just like it was supposed to be. Wednesday afternoon when I returned from work, I saw six different building employees, all coincidentally very close to my size, wearing very familiar clothing. ("Hey, I have a shirt just like that.") I didn't really worry about it until Friday afternoon when my laundry did not come back. I'm a little slow after a long work week.

Obviously, it was time to go out on my own into the dark, cruel world of doing my own laundry. My girlfriend happened to be visiting while I was doing my first couple loads.

After some quiet observation, she politely bellowed, "*What the hell are you doing?*"

"Laundry, dear heart, love of my life. Why do you ask?" I answered sweetly.

"Did you even think about sorting those? You have a white towel in with a pair of dark denim jeans, for crying out loud."

Ha! I had her. "Well, of *course* I sorted them, sweetie-pie-schnookums-teddy-bear. The clothes in the washer are dirty, and the clothes still on the floor in my room are clean. Did you really think, cuddle-cozy-pooh-bear, that I would *not* sort them? I am, as you know, independent."

For some reason, she about lost it. Apparently, in her book I had committed a really serious sin, right up there with murder, adultery, and God *forbid* not having matching sheets on my bed (another story altogether). She began to spout about whites versus colors, delicates, and something called "permanent press," which to that point I had only thought of as a basketball term. She named some woman called "Polly Ester" who had a hard time being washed with cotton, which made no sense to me, as I wash with water. She got on her soapbox (actually, it was my soapbox) about detergents and fabric softeners and dryer sheets. By that time I had already been berated into just nodding my head and saying, "Yes, dear one," a lot. No amount of clean clothes was worth this.

I am still doing my own laundry, and in doing so am bringing all my clothes gradually into one shade of pinkish brown. Whenever I see my girlfriend, I wear my Navy uniform because they are cleaned professionally, and also so she doesn't see that all my other clothes are becoming the same color. Three years from now, I will have no trouble deciding what to wear in the morning, as everything will look very much alike. I'm actually looking forward to the simplicity.

The Importance of Matching Sheets

More girlfriend stuff. I am still *facing this issue with my mom, but I have learned that it is more due to my ignorance than her persistence. I'm glad she loves me anyway.*

❧   ❧   ❧

People have always told me that I am fairly bright. I never believed them, but that was the popular opinion. I graduated from a fairly rigorous university with an engineering degree (meaning that I fooled the Dean in addition to the general public) and proceeded with life. In my newly furnished apartment in my new bedroom on my new bed I placed … sheets. Not old sheets or new sheets or colored sheets or sheets of plastic or sheets with Cookie Monster on them, just sheets; whatever I could get from my grandmother and mom that would fit on my bed. After all, I *sleep* on sheets, and that usually involves closing my eyes and turning out the lights, so it really doesn't matter what is on my bed, right?

Well, apparently not. My girlfriend upon her very first visit asked me when I was going to get matching sheets. I replied quite seriously sometime between when Hell froze over and the Orioles won the pennant *and* didn't trade anyone. I was of course slapped and verbally berated for not realizing the necessity of having matching color schemes at night in the dark with my eyes closed.

"No, stupid," she explained, using what she thought that was my given name, "They are for when others come to visit, so everything looks neat and organized." She actually said this to someone who has difficulty organizing a sock drawer, and even more difficulty in seeing why matching socks are really that important anyway. I *like* disorganization. It adds a certain randomness to life.

"But dear, then why did you make me buy that huge overstuffed comforter?" which, I didn't add, covers my bed, my pillows, my night table, my clock radio, my desk, and still spills out into the hallway if I don't fold it just right.

"Oh, Rob," she rolled her eyes, "you *need* matching sheets, and that's that." Well, that settled *that* little matter. It was obvious that my beloved thought that my life was going straight into the toilet without passing go if I did not get the top sheet and the pillow cases to match. So three hours and 87 dollars and 63 cents later, I was the proud owner of an ugly set of lime green sheets with white stripes and pink flowers near the corners. They were on sale.

I learned some lessons that day. Sheets are overpriced. My girlfriend has horrible taste in bed linens. Sheet stores are pretty boring. You can't actually throw sheets on a bed and take them on a test drive around Snoozeville, and you can't wrap yourself like a mummy or anything. All in all, a pretty dull time.

Though beaten, I was determined to make the most of it. I called my mom and told her that I had finally, of my own volition, bought matching sheets. She was so proud that when she recovered she asked when I was going to get a dust ruffle.

I replied sometime after the Bucs won the Super Bowl and pigs not only flew but did so without disrupting regular airline traffic. My girlfriend slapped me. She also rearranged my socks. There is no justice.

Why I'm Banished from Victoria's Secret

As true as it is short ...

❦　　　❦　　　❦

There are certain members of the male population who say that they understand women. I am not one of those members. In my own humble opinion, those men who boast that they do understand women are either:

a) gods

or most likely

b) complete and total liars.

There is almost no aspect of the female species that does not confuse me. Hair, makeup, soap operas, the list goes on.

The thing that gives me the biggest headache concerning the fairer sex is lingerie. This entire concept baffles me. If I understand correctly, the entire idea behind lingerie is that when you put it on, it makes you and your partner so steamy that you want to take it off immediately. To a person who prides himself on logic and efficiency, this makes no sense. You do not buy shoes that hurt so bad you want to take them off immediately. You do not buy a dinner that tastes so bad that you want to stop eating as soon as you taste it. Besides this completely illogical basis for existence, lingerie is very expensive, considering it is made of mostly see-through stuff and some wire.

Being the modern, hip type of guy that I am, I tried to play along. I actually went in to one of the better known lingerie chains to buy something for my girlfriend. "Fish out of water" is woefully inadequate to describe this experience. This absolute goddess of a saleswoman walks up, smiles, and purrs "Can I help you?" In her mind I could hear her saying, "This boy needs serious help."

I replied, as calmly as I could, "I-I-I w-w-w-wwwant t-t-to buy som-something mmmy girlfriend for."

"Pardon me?" said goddess woman.

"Girlfriend. Buy something. Nice."

"Oh, OK. I got it. This is your first time."

My mind immediately thought "Oh, no, of course not. I am in here every other day. Don't be silly. I understand women." However, the bridge on the road from my brain to my mouth went out under a sensual overload, and all that came out was some grunting noises. Then I drooled. I was impressing the heck out of goddess woman.

She smelled a commission, though, and she plunged on. "What size is she?" I thought this over for a moment. Size? Small? Petite? Medium? A brilliant inspiration popped into my head. I put my hand out, about five feet and four inches off the floor, smiled, and said, "She is about this size, I think." Wrong answer. Goddess woman, commission be damned, cursed, called me a cretin, insulted my parentage, kicked me in the shin, and left. I limped out of the store, vowing never to attempt this foolishness again. Let her come to bed in sweats and a tee shirt, like me. I used the money to take her to Pizza Hut and the new Schwarzenegger flick instead. And people say I am not romantic.

Christmas in Gingerbread Hell

I think this is the best of the girlfriend stories. The following happened about ten years ago, and almost every word of this is true.

❦   ❦   ❦

Last Christmas my lovely and wonderful girlfriend decided that it would be nice if she and I spent some quality time "bonding." I agreed, and immediately suggested covering our bodies with chocolate sauce and sticking ourselves to each other. She politely corrected me. "No, you cretin. Let's do something creative and wonderful and incredibly time consuming. Let's build a gingerbread house."

For those of you not familiar with the idea, the basic premise as explained to me by the love of my life is that you spend approximately two lunar months and about $71.48 constructing this masterpiece of culinary architecture, and then you give it away. This made no sense to me, and I said as much. She rewarded my honesty by threatening to drop the mixer down my shorts. It's hard to argue with that kind of logic.

We proceeded to begin construction. Step one was to mix the gingerbread dough. This was done with maximum mess and maximum violence. First, I got smacked for tasting the dough a few (12) times. Then, when I tried to sneak out to go do something both safer and more exciting, like rearranging my underwear drawer, she got a little confused about what or whom to use the rolling pin on.

With my escape thwarted, and my lack of enthusiasm resolved, (the threat of blunt trauma does wonders for my motivation), we continued upon our endeavor. We rolled the dough into sheets, which would have been of uniform thickness, except that they weren't, and applied the provided templates. These were supposed to provide us with four similar walls, two identical pieces of gingerbread for the roof, and pieces for the steeple. They instead provided us with seventeen pieces that were similar only in that they were all made of gingerbread. It was less and less likely that our gingerbread creation would ever resemble the majestic steeped creation on the box. In fact, it was less and less likely that our gingerbread creation would ever resemble anything that would be even close to habitable, even by gingerbread people standards. After I pointed this out, it was, however, more and more likely that I would be sleeping on the couch until July.

According to the directions, we were supposed to assemble the pieces of our little cottage with "small spoonfuls of confectioner's sugar." Yeah, right. No real man would use "small spoonfuls" of anything during a construction job. It may be gingerbread, but it's still a house. I began to load up the caulking gun. My wonderful, loving girlfriend began loading up her father's Winchester. I'm a better shot, but I was slightly outgunned, so in the end, we went with the spoonfuls of sugar. As I suspected, the sugar was totally inadequate. It was two steps to the left of useless for joining anything, so I suggested crazy glue. The princess suggested Bellevue.

Eventually, we succeeded in creating something resembling a structure that looked somewhat like a church if you looked at it the right way, like with your eyes closed. At this point, I was no longer confused on *why* we would want to give this thing away.

After we finally got it to stand on its own (*important note*: cardboard and gingerbread are the same color), it was time to decorate it with candy. This turned out to be pretty easy, as I kept two very important tenets in mind:

1. the more you sample, the less you actually have to waste on the house.

2. symmetry is unimportant to gingerbread people.

The last step was to create a gingerbread congregation to celebrate in our gingerbread church. After much deliberation, we made a very professional community consisting of gingerbread lawyers, gingerbread doctors, gingerbread fighter pilots, and even a gingerbread President of the United States. My girlfriend was very proud of our creation, and asked my opinion on a name. I politely suggested "First Church of the Amazons," as by some accident *all* the members of the congregation except the gingerbread janitor were women. She politely suggested I look into having a relationship by myself.

Finally finished, she asked where we should put it until it was time to give it away to the "lucky" recipients. I suggested anywhere that it could not be reasonably associated with us.

In the end, she was so pleased with our masterpiece, she ended up keeping it. She did, however, give me away.

Dave and his Future Ex-Wife

"We pause from the girlfriend stories to bring you this exclusive roommate story ..." Dave and "my girlfriend" sort of co-existed in my life. Dave and I are still lifelong friends; "she" is married to someone else and we are out of each other's lives. There's a lesson there somewhere.

Anyway, the following was inspired when Dave met his future ex-wife.

❋　　　　❋　　　　❋

Women do funny things to guys. It is truly amazing to watch. One week a guy is a perfectly normal, functioning male organism that prepares frozen food, cleans the apartment monthly, and is at least aware of what a washing machine is used for. And the next week, he is, well, *not*. He has met *her*, and now that he has met *her*, his life is forever changed. Because of *her*, he showers everyday. Because of *her*, he actually irons. Because of *her*, he uses silverware. All the pillars of male bachelorhood are smashed forever, or at least until he gets dumped. A good example of this phenomenon is my roommate, or at least what used to be my roommate.

My roommate used to be the typical male bachelor, and together we formed a typical roommate duo. We drank together, were ignored by women together, fell down together, all the usual things. Then he met *Sharon*, and my roommate, once a strong, intelligent, model example of the American bachelor, was reduced to a panting, drooling block of protoplasm with less free will than an amoeba. Few amoebas are as well trained, however.

Our typical conversations used to cover all the normal male subjects. Bikinis, sports, bikini models, frozen food, bikinis, and occasionally, the weather.

"Hope it doesn't rain today. No bikinis." Now our conversations are typically a little more one sided.

ME: Hey, bud, how was work?

HIM (in a somewhat zombie-like tone): Sharon.

ME: Hmm. Bears are on tonight. Gonna watch?

HIM: Sharon.

ME: OK. Your underwear is on fire.

HIM: Sharon.

He tries to put on a macho act. He wears turtlenecks all the time so no one can see the dog collar, and swears up and down that she will do whatever he says. This is, at least, a true statement. She will do whatever he says, but only because she tells him ahead of time what he is allowed to say.

To illustrate how far my roommate has fallen off of the bachelor wagon, I will demonstrate how this obviously *very special* female has come between him and that most sacred bachelor tradition; professional football.

To say that my roommate and I are just "football fans" is about the same as saying that pizza is just a food and beer just a beverage. We *define* the term "professional football fan." Look it up, and you will find us, slamming chicken wings and guzzling beer. We begin looking forward to the weekend games about 17 seconds after the Monday night game ends, and it is all we talk about all week. Or at least it used to be (refer to conversation above).

Now, because Sharon does not really *like* football (which should be a crime punishable by a life sentence of watching endless Oprah reruns), he spends his Sundays either being dragged around the mall or watching 1980's movies, which would be premiering except for the fact that they have already been on 22 times. He will, of course, insist that this is totally his idea. "Molly Ringwold is really a talented actress," he says.

Now, it is all fine and good to make sacrifices for the woman you love. Time, money, a kidney, OK, but this is *professional football*. I am thoroughly convinced that God in His infinite wisdom created Sundays for professional football, and the only reason He gave us the off-season is to make us appreciate this great gift. Furthermore, He is an avid fan, though not of Buffalo. No way could a team with that much talent lose the Super Bowl four times in a row. I am sure He runs a pool among the angels. Having thus stated my beliefs, it is easy to see why I find it impossible to believe that my roommate allows *her* to come between him and football. Now, I love my girlfriend, but if she even attempted to interrupt the *divine purpose* of Sunday, I can guarantee that my love for her would not prevent me from bribing her to leave. If the Bears were on, my love for her would not prevent me from locking her in the garage.

I don't see much of my roommate anymore. Last weekend he did something fun without Sharon for about seventy-two seconds, so now she is punishing him by taking him to her mother's for the weekend.

I would like to point out that I will go to my girlfriend's mother's house anytime provided it is in the off season.

Why Men Should Not Do Aerobics

I did try aerobics, and actually not only enjoyed it, but was fairly good at it too. But that came later. The first few times went pretty much as described below.

❋   ❋   ❋

There are certain things in this world that men were just not intended to do. Changing diapers, eating tofu, and baking casseroles certainly fall into this category. However, there is an activity which mere mortal males should avoid with even greater trepidation—aerobics.

I am quite qualified to speak on this subject, because at this very moment I can move no part of my lower body, and this is entirely due to aerobics. I am quite sure I have a lower body, because from it emanates pain equal to that of non-sedated testicle removal. I just have no control over it.

This started two weeks ago, when at the polite request of my girlfriend I enrolled in an aerobics class. "Exercise, Fat Boy, or I am leaving you," was how she put it. Wanting to show off and be macho and all that other idiot guy stuff, I signed up for not just any aerobics class, but *step* aerobics. Little did I know that step aerobics is two notches higher on the pain meter than regular aerobics, which itself is seventeen notches above the impact associated with falling out of a twelve-story window. Not only that, but I talked one of my co-workers, Al, into signing up with me, and he swears that he will kill me just as soon as he can stand up without assistance.

To put it plainly, I *hurt*. Very much. Whatever I did to offend the gods or Jane Fonda I am very sorry, because now when I tell my legs to move they reply that they are on strike. I am not used to having body parts disobey orders, and when they do, life becomes *very* difficult. Try attempting to use the bathroom in the middle of the night when your legs *do not function.*

Please notice that I did not say that all guys should not do aerobics. I said *mere mortal* men should not attempt aerobics. My instructor happens to be male, and though many of you are probably snickering under you breath at a male aerobics instructor, you would stop fifty-eight seconds into the workout, and your heart would probably stop soon after.

This guy is a killer, and obviously immortal as no normal human could survive this. After what seemed like an eternity, during which I had sweated off thirteen pounds, the instructor halted the class. I wanted to cheer now that we were finished, but couldn't find the breath. While I was still looking for it, he bellowed, "Now that we are warmed up, let's get started."

We hopped. We jumped. We spun. We stepped. We attempted maneuvers that could prove fatal to the rhythmically challenged such as me. At one point, I looked to Al for encouragement, and he had, in his enthusiasm, gotten his arm stuck behind his head, which was now twisted approximately 237 degrees. His legs were also tangled, and one of his feet stuck out at an odd angle. When I offered him assistance, he told me that the minute he was untangled he was going to bludgeon me to death with the eighty-year-old man in the row ahead of him. Incidentally, this octogenarian could probably have kicked both our asses. I withdrew my offer of assistance and tripped him instead.

Two eternities later, class ended. By this point I was completely unable to move, and had to be helped off the floor and into my car, where I sat for two hours trying to muster the strength to turn the ignition. Deciding that no woman could possibly be worth this amount of pain, I told my girlfriend to accept me as I was or leave. She listened long enough to decide to do neither, and then settled on torturing me by poking me wherever it hurt, which was everywhere.

I have decided that I will probably live longer if I refrain from exercising, and even longer if I refrain from listening to my girlfriend because deep down she is trying to kill me.

A somewhat less important but equally painful lesson learned here was that you should never, *never* apply Ben-Gay to your entire body. Unfortunately, I did not learn this in time to tell Al, which may have something to do with the lawsuit he has filed.

Goodness, Gracious my Roommate's on Fire!

My favorite Dave story. I love him to death, but he can't barbecue without hurting himself. We still talk about this …

❁   ❁   ❁

There are several things my roommate does well. For example, he can get slapped by 17 different women at the local singles bar, whereas I have only been able to get slapped by 12. He also makes *the* best whiskey sour I have ever tasted. These two superior qualities help me to overlook his sole fault; his inability to barbecue with anything resembling safety.

When it comes to grill skills, my roommate is perhaps the most untalented, ungifted, un-flame-retardant person on this planet. In him, the quest for food collides with the quest for fire, and the resulting smoke and flame have earned my roommate the dubious title "Most Likely to Spontaneously Combust."

His ineptitude is not from lack of practice. At least three times a week (according to the local fire inspector) we attempt to barbecue on the grill his mother purchased for us. It is a truly beautiful grill, with an automatic lighter, two separate burners, and all the grill space two bachelors could possibly need. We could with little effort barbecue a brontosaurus if we wanted to, provided we could find one this late in the season. It even has a fire extinguisher and a built-in first aid kit, both of which receive regular use.

The first hurdle we must overcome each time we embark on our quest for hamburger is the actual lighting of the grill. This is accomplished by opening the gas valve, turning on the burners, pushing the "auto-light" button 32 times, and then going to get a match.

Every night my roommate goes and gets the match, and every night he forgets to open the grill before lighting it, and so every night we experience an explosion not quite equivalent to a five-hundred-pound bomb. Currently we have one eyebrow between us, and exactly six arm hairs.

Once the grill is lit and the burn salve applied, we place a piece of tin foil down on the grill, and then it is time to begin cooking our dinner. As we are bachelors, we are very selective about what we eat. Our grillable meat must meet three very stringent criteria.

1.   It must be dead.

2.   It must be cheap.

3.   It must not be able to be linked to any of our neighbors' missing pets.

With these demanding standards met, we begin to grill. Approximately two minutes after this evolution begins, my roommate attempts to turn the meat using a spatula, or a snow shovel if the spatula is in the dishwasher. At this point, the tin foil invariably ignites. Now, I have double checked, but nowhere on the tin foil box is there a flammable warning of any sort. Furthermore, after 28 attempts with first a lighter and then a blowtorch, I have been unable to get tin foil to do anything but melt. I have determined that my roommate has some special gift which enables him to do this *every time he barbecues.*

Upon foil ignition, my roommate lets loose a stream of profanity which would make a sailor blush as he jumps around beating the flames back with the spatula. I stand by with the fire extinguisher ready to back him up as necessary. Eventually, one or the other of us remembers that fire needs oxygen to survive, and if we put the lid down, we might just starve those flames back to something more manageable. As we do this, we congratulate ourselves once again for failing to ignite, while great clouds of smoke begin to billow out and obscure visibility for miles around. This is when our neighbors close their doors and coincides exactly with when the people who live upstairs go out for dinner.

We have this problem no matter what we our grilling. I have scientifically concluded that this is because our grill is possessed. You could put a damp piece of bread on our grill, close the lid, and somehow within about three minutes great clouds of smoke will begin billowing out. There are evil smoke spirits in our grill, and they are out to get my roommate and me, and that is that.

I casually asked, after one of our more "exciting" experiences involving two different fire departments and more carbon dioxide than what is produced daily by the population of Cleveland, where he learned to barbecue. He replied through his bandages, "Moomphfweeesertmeeef," which I knew meant "My father taught me."

Now, I did not believe there could be two people in the world that barbecue-ingly challenged, and when his family came to visit, I found out I was right. His father is not as bad as my roommate, *he is worse*.

Not only did he need to use the match *and* forget to raise the lid before lighting, the tin foil actually ignited *in his hands*. He then proceeded to achieve meltdown unseen since Chernobyl (although this one was not radioactive, we think). Here are men truly beyond help.

Despite his and his father's best efforts, my roommate and I are still alive and reasonably non-crispy. He is about to be married, and I am buying him a microwave. If he tries to trade it in for a new grill, I may shoot him.

Water Skiing Can Kill You

Dave and I on the high seas.

❦　　　　❦　　　　❦

Most people assume that because I am in the Navy, I have at least a casual acquaintance with water. In fact, my naval experience has taught me to be very comfortable in and around water, and have always enjoyed two of the most popular pool/beach activities—swimming and babe-ogling.

All this changed when I tried to learn a new water sport: water-skiing. I had seen this done on TV and in the movies any number of times. To the best of my knowledge, a scantily clad female wearing cool sunglasses pulls a sun-tanned male with even cooler sunglasses behind a very fast, very expensive boat. The boat is usually painted red with some kind of provocative name like "Luscious" or "Exotica." It is adequately stocked with cold beer and hot women, and there is good food and a really loud radio. The guy being towed pops right up on the ski, does tricks, and never falls off. Piece of cake, I thought. I can do this.

My roommate provided the boat. It was neither very expensive nor very fast. It was not painted any shade of red (unless rust counts) and it was affectionately named "The Floating Coffin." This name had won out over "Shark-bait." Our food supply consisted of three warm beers and a half-eaten Twinkie. We had no women, hot or otherwise. We did have one of our friends along, who slept virtually the entire time, waking only long enough to eat the half Twinkie, drink a beer, and burp loudly. We had a heated discussion on whether or not he would make a good anchor. Our sunglasses were not cool, and (we found this out sooner rather than later) they sank. Already, things were significantly different from the picture I had painted for myself, and I hadn't even gotten wet yet.

When I finally did get in the water, I learned that one does not get right up on water skis. Apparently there is a requirement that first one must get dragged on one's face through the water at 20 knots at least 24 or 25 times. "Knot" is nautical terminology; it means "not quite equal to miles per hour," but it's still pretty damn fast. It was definitely a learning experience. On my second try I learned my sunglasses sink. My fourth, I learned my bathing suit needs to be tied better. Try seven taught me that it is better to let go of the rope sooner than later. Try nineteen taught me to find a new water sport.

Finally, the moment came. For six whole seconds, I was actually up on the skis, balanced, and in control of my own wave-skimming destiny. Then all Hell broke loose. The next ten seconds saw me do all those tricks the really good water skiers are known for; one leg, 360s, holding the rope with your toes, splits, jumps, etc. Mind you, I was *not* showing off, I was just trying to stay on the damned skis. This eventually proved impossible, and my impact with the water was as spectacular as it was violent. Observers would later liken it to a wounded aircraft crashing into the water and cart wheeling across the surface. I immediately likened it to being hit by a truck.

To make matters worse, my roommate did not see me go down, and I bobbed around for twenty minutes until he realized I was no longer there. Wanting to make up for lost time, he came looking for me at full throttle. This is when we learned that speedboats in general do *not* stop on a dime. This speedboat, in particular, was prepared to stop on *me*. Even drunk, babe-ogling was never this dangerous.

I have decided it is in my best interest not to attempt more water-skiing. It is also in my best interest never to let my roommate tow me behind any type of vehicle ever again. I am going back to babe ogling. It's less physically demanding, less costly, and potentially more rewarding. While it is doubtful I will be any more successful, at least it is certain I will be much more uninjured.

It's a good thing I am not in the Air Force. I don't even want to think about the damage I could do to myself trying to learn hang-gliding.

Bachelors, Cable TV, and Understanding Sex

I think I might have had a few cocktails before I wrote this one.

❦   ❦   ❦

It was a Saturday night, and my roommate and I were sitting on the couch watching TV. I could try and make up an excuse for this, but the fact of the matter is his fiancé was in the kitchen and his leash was only long enough to get him into the living room. As for me, I just didn't feel like going out, primarily because none of the 37 women I asked did either.

As we were flipping through the channels, one of the educational stations was airing a program titled, "Understanding Sex." This is a title guaranteed to catch the attention of any bachelor, whether or not he is even in the same room as the TV, and we responded in typical bachelor fashion by cheering and hooting and making armpit noises. Bachelors have a lot in common with fifth graders when it comes to discussing the "s-word."

It is a proven fact that while guys think about sex only at certain times, like when they are breathing, they will leap at the chance to learn more about this mystical topic. For some men, it comes from a deep-seated thirst for educational knowledge. For others (approximately 99.8 percent), it comes from the desire to improve their chances of getting horizontal with anything in a skirt that does not try to kill them. My roommate and I fit into this second category, and eagerly awaited the end of the commercial break in hopes of seeing sweating bodies and tips on how we can prolong our sexual experiences to at least three minutes.

We were sorely disappointed. This documentary insisted on relating how all sorts of beings reproduce, from flowers to insects to mammals to eventually humans. We also learned that there are several asexual species, such as amoebas, whip tail lizards, and Richard Simmons, and they are all female. Apparently, these species were perfectly happy without any males around, although the grass in front of the lizard homes was rather long, and their cars did not run. I can speak only for myself and my roommate (who, since his recent engagement, is not allowed to speak for himself), but we are not at all interested in the mating habits of lizards or three-toed tree sloths. While this information was educational and maybe even useful ("Alex, I'll take mating habits of small lizards for eight hundred."), it did nothing to slate our hormonal thirsts. Adding insult to injury, we were informed that approximately 90 percent of the animal kingdom, including the platypus, which we always make fun of, was more sexually active than we were. Thank God for cable.

As if that wasn't enough, the female narrator cheerily explained how the entire sex process was pretty much female dominated. While males need only be alive in order to want to have sex, females are slightly more selective. This I had already learned for myself. After exhaustive field research, I have determined that females want to have sex approximately once every other solar eclipse, and then only if it falls on a Friday.

To support the narrator's point, the following experiment was cited.

Apparently, a dominant female gorilla called "Hillary Clinton" was taken from her native habitat called "the Bronx" and taught to communicate with sign language. (Being able to communicate at all put her ahead of most inhabitants of the Bronx, or even New York City, for that matter.) When the time was right, she was exposed to several different suitable male gorillas and asked to comment. She referred to one lucky suitor as "a toilet," and another as "Gilbert Godfrey." Had this male suitor understood what the Hell Hillary Clinton was saying, he would have been scarred for life. As it was, he just beat his chest and ate a banana and tried to mate with an artificial tree. Finally, she picked a mate, and then spent the next two years alternately ignoring him and beating the living banana out of him, as is a woman's prerogative.

And I thought the bar scene was rough.

Cindy Brady and the Evils of Nickel Beer Night

This story has everything (well, it's a little short on facts, but other than that). My trusty roommate Dave, excessive alcohol consumption, young women, nuns, a goat, and a wooden Indian. "I'll never drink again ..."

❄   ❄   ❄

Oh, boy. I did it again. Nickel beer night at the local beer-hall-slash-meat-market. Somebody get me a doctor. There is a very small very angry man with a very large very loud jackhammer doing demolition work in my cranial cavity. Meanwhile, there is more cotton in my mouth than in both Carolinas. I went to bed with Cindy Crawford, but I woke up with Cindy Brady. I don't remember anything that happened after about my seventh beer, especially concerning the fire hydrant in my living room and the goat tied to my front stoop, but based upon past experiences and a few painful shards of memory, the evening went something like this.

As usual, my roommate and I embarked upon our beer guzzling skirt-chasing-testosterone-overflowing ritual by heading for Nickel Beer Night. There are few things on earth that young bachelors hold more sacred than cheap cold beer. The only one I can think of off the top of my head is *free* cold beer, but a nickel a pop is close, and at that price it is tough to go wrong. We arrived, pocket full of nickels, and my roommate ordered his first beer. I ordered my first four, because it was his turn to drive. Big shot that I am, I dropped a quarter on the bar to pay for the first round.

We bumped into two of my roommate's friends. They, like him, were U.S. Marines, normally defined as loud, uncultured, slightly psychotic creatures that excel at violence, reducing third world pissant I-want-to-make-trouble nations into parking lots, and cutting each other's hair *really* short. Thirty-seven dollars and fifty-five cents later, we engaged in our first female acquisition exercise of the evening. My roommate made a valiant effort with a very attractive female specimen, but got flamed and went down hard. Luckily, he landed in his beer, and recovered quickly. Marine friend number one, slightly intoxicated, was putting the moves on a target which he at least thought was female, but that outweighed any two of us and was chewing tobacco. Marine friend number two, slightly more intoxicated, was putting the moves on a wooden Indian. After ten minutes of intense conversation, he came to the table and reported that because he had not yet been slapped or told to copulate with a rock he thought he had a good shot of hooking up. Rather than crush his spirits by telling him he was in love with an antique, we wished him luck and off he went.

I was hanging back, like a surfer just waiting for that perfect wave. Truth be told, in my present overly inebriated state, I couldn't handle a warm bath much less a perfect wave, but that didn't stop me. My roommate and I proceeded to get shot down by eleven women in the space of about nine minutes, including two waitresses, a nun, a grandmother, and a life size poster of Kathy Ireland. We pulled back to regroup, refill, and re-evaluate.

While we were in conference, two females took pity on us and walked over. Being that I was seeing life through six sets of beer goggles, the girl talking to me was *the* most beautiful woman in the bar. Later I would find out that she would have been the second most beautiful woman in a room by herself. My roommate, being much closer to sober, recognized the situation for what it was and tried to warn me off. I think his exact words were "We need to leave now. One of them looks like George Foreman and the other one just ate a barstool." I would hear none of it, so my loyal roommate, in a moment of both ingenuity and desperation, feigned death until the girls got the message and excused themselves.

After the departure of the Gruesome Twosome, my memory goes blank, so I can't explain Cindy Brady, the goat, or the fire hydrant, and any attempt would be pure fiction. Apparently, it is a pretty good story, because my roommate hasn't stopped shaking his head or laughing.

Damage control starts this morning. After a bottle and a half of aspirin, I plan to drive to the nearest fire station and return the hydrant via the "dump the body out of the moving car" method, and then set the goat free in my neighbors' yard. After Cindy goes to school, of course. For some reason I really don't want to think about, she is very attached to that goat.

Wedding Bells and Boxing Gloves

There is a huge difference between a "couple" and a "couple planning to get married." I certainly appreciate this more today than I did when I wrote this. The infamous "girlfriend" makes a brief appearance in here too.

❋   ❋   ❋

Two of my very close friends are planning to get married. I say *planning to get married* because they are driving each other nuts with preparation plans, and I'm not really sure they will still be in love when the wedding day does finally get here. Actually, I am not sure they will even be speaking to each other.

To say they are making extensive plans would be an incredible understatement. I don't think the US made as many plans during World War II as they are making for their wedding.

First they had to register. Now, when I was young, I was taught that unless asked, you never came right out and said what you wanted to be given for such-and-such an occasion, so registering is kind of lost on me, and I refuse to participate. If I feel so inclined, I will buy the happy couple a lamp in the shape of a female leg complete with fishnet stocking and lovely orange and purple polka-dotted lampshade, and *dammit* they better be grateful. This has caused a serious disagreement between my girlfriend and I about the wedding gift—she wants to buy the bride a leash and the groom a collar. She went to an all girl college; does it show?

Next they had to find a church. They were rather dismayed when all the churches they looked at had some sort of crazy stipulation about not living together before the marriage. My pal the groom, being the practical fellow that he is, said, "Ah, don't worry about it. We'll just lie." I don't want to be anywhere near him when he says "I do," the lightning shows up, and from on high you hear God's voice: "I think you already DID!"

Caterers, musicians, reception hall, the list goes on. Who needs it? Watching them slowly go insane over this made me decide to formulate my own wedding plans now so that when I meet that certain special female, I am ready.

For the actual ceremony, we will go to a church one Saturday and wait for someone else's wedding. When the time for the vows comes up, me and my future Mrs. will jump up, shout "I do!" and run like Hell before anyone can catch us. I will throw rice at her on the way out for effect. For the reception we will reserve a McDonald's; sort of like a birthday party, but with better presents. I own a radio and some CD's, so that takes care of music. For the honeymoon I will get us a room at Motel 6 for three days. I think I even have a coupon for a free continental breakfast.

I am thoroughly convinced that this short, sweet, and very sincere plan is the way to go. Some call me unromantic, but I call it practical. I will have enough to worry about getting her to put up with me through the marriage; I don't need to worsen my chances by asking her to put up with me through the wedding preparation, too. Besides, I really like McDonald's. As the guest of honor, I would even get a free hat.

Golf is a Four Letter Word

For years I hated golf. To me, it was boring, expensive, and a symbol of the elderly. My opinions have changed, and this story was written when I was trying to make that transition from golf-hater to respectable duffer. It has turned out to be a much longer transition than I had anticipated, but at least my escapades on the course have provided comic relief for hundreds of other, better golfers.

❋   ❋   ❋

Hundreds of years ago, the brilliant people of Scotland gave us the game of golf. While I am sure they thought they were providing a useful contribution to the world of sports, millions of badly dressed handicappers are still suffering from this tragedy today.

I would like to ask anyone of Scottish descent who might be reading just *what in* the *Hell were your kilt-wearing-bagpipe-playing ancestors thinking when they came up with this?* Were they really that desperate for something to do? Couldn't they read maps? England, Wales, Ireland, they were all right there. If the Scots were that bored, they should have invaded something. Look at the Germans. They were left unoccupied (literally) for all of five minutes before they decided to invade France *twice*. They did *not* invent a game that requires you to dress plaid-ly and swing at a ridiculously small ball with a club (Historical Note: Germans have always had more important things to do with clubs).

Unfortunately, that was the past. The present is that as a junior naval officer, I am expected to be somewhat familiar with and capable of playing the game of golf. Sadly, this meant that I was forced to use my golf clubs for something other than driving nails or threatening my neighbor.

I began my pursuit of golf excellence on the driving range. I had a borrowed club; (a driver, appropriate for said driving range), a bucket of balls, and a really snazzy golf shirt. The shirt was the only thing I was reasonably confident I could use correctly. I did not, however, have a tee. Apparently, this is a small device one places the ball on at the driving range, in order to look professional and otherwise competent. This fact I learned this from a twelve-year-old who was trying really hard not to laugh at me.

Having finally secured (stolen) a tee, I was ready to begin. My grandfather had spent hours trying to teach me the correct way to swing a golf club, and I did a few warm-up swings that I hoped were a good approximation. Then I placed the ball on the tee, lined up, took a deep breath, crossed myself, and began my backswing. I froze in that position, club drawn back, knees slightly bent, eyes on the ball. One noble thought popped into mind as I was about to enter the brotherhood of this great game. "Oh my God this hurts! How can any sane person do this on purpose?"

I closed my eyes and swung. What a mighty swing it was, too. I could hear the club rip through the air, followed by the *thwack* of contact with the ball. I opened my eyes and saw the tee fluttering back to earth as splinters. Another lesson learned; tees are disposable. I also located the ball, three feet forward and slightly to the left of where I had teed it up. This was a less than impressive start.

Undaunted, I tried again. And again. And again. I learned all kinds of new words from people around me who were watching me make a fool of myself. Slice and hook were two favorites. Some guy named Mulligan was mentioned a lot, too. At one point I actually stunned and amazed my audience by somehow hitting the ball fifteen feet *behind* me. This was about the time I figured out I could throw the damn ball farther than I could ever hit it. This is also about the time I figured out that the only way I would ever be mentioned in the same breath as Jack Nicklaus was if I beat him to death with a six-iron, since I'll be damned if I know what else to do with it anyway.

Finally, I teed up my next to last ball. I drew back, closed my eyes, and prepared to let loose. "Stand in front of him, it's the safest place!" one of my disciples yelled. That did it! I imparted all my rage and anger at being forced into this nightmarish "game" into the most devastating swing ever imagined. The club head whipped around like it had a personal vendetta against the ball. *Crack!* I opened my eyes, and almost fainted. The ball was actually in the air. I had hit a descent drive.

In time, this drive ended, as all drives do. The ball landed about two hundred twenty five yards down range. Not a pro shot by any means, but nine times farther than I had hit any other shot all day, and this one went *straight*.

Still in shock, I teed up my last ball. I tried to mimic everything I did on the previous shot; the backswing, the swing, the follow through. Could I do it? Could I hit that stupid white ball an unbelievable two times in a row? I took a deep breath, I drew back, and I let it fly …

When I awoke in the hospital, they tried to explain to me what happened. Apparently, I swung so hard I missed the ball entirely, and clocked myself in the head with the club. My immediate reaction was to begin to throttle the doctor, because he looked Scottish and therefore was at least partially responsible.

After I was restrained and heavily sedated, I had a nice long talk with the resident psychiatrist. He said I should consider another hobby. Then he had to leave to make his tee time.

Damn those Scots.

Big Italian Weddings
(complete with big Italians)

Previously, we have discussed my feelings towards weddings, and also my less-than-extensive plans for my own wedding. This story is sort of related, as it deals with some of the family weddings I have been exposed to. Maybe subconsciously this is why I was single for so long.

❋   ❋   ❋

There are few things that I can think of that are louder than a big Italian wedding; World War II and the daycare center behind my building are the only two that come to mind right away. I should know, too. There are a lot of big Italians in my family.

I have nine aunts and uncles between my parents, and, in the Italian tradition, dozens of cousins and more second and removed and twice removed but still living here cousins than one person should legally be allowed. (What is "removed," anyway? They are here, I can see them, I have to be nice to them, where were they "removed" to?) My family averages about two weddings a year between the two sides, counting second marriages and "life-partnerships." No matter which side it is, we get to go. What a blessing *that* is.

This means that twice a year I must put on a suit *on a weekend* and go to a large structure filled with people I haven't seen since the last time there was an unexplained pregnancy involving someone on this particular side of the family. For reference, I keep close to whichever parent belongs to the side of the family responsible for bringing us here. As an example:

ME: Psst, Dad, who is that?

DAD: How should I know? We only see them twice a year, tops.

ME: Thanks Dad.

DAD: Go bother your mother, son.

After the ceremony, we all go to the reception. This means open bar, which alleviates my suffering a little. I always go looking for the happy couple for two reasons. First, to see if they are still happy: one of my cousins actually had his first marital spat in the limo on the way to the reception. This was his fault—he shouldn't have brought a date. Second, I want to see if they tried to hide and start the honeymoon early. Another of my cousins did that. He was less than happy to see me.

At the reception, the main event is watching the elder and esteemed members of my family get hammered. I mean smashed, loaded, blotto, wasted, *gone*. Upon accomplishing this goal, they seek me out to give me advice on what to them is the most difficult stage of life. "Stop and smell the roses, because when the going gets tough, you can't make him drink. That's what I always say." Yeah, thanks, good to see you. Have another gin and tonic, and then go dance with the coat rack.

My favorite part of the wedding (besides when we get to leave) is the cake cutting ceremony. This ancient tradition encompasses all the aspects of marriage in my family; smiles, playfulness, knife wielding spouses, and food on the front of the groom's clothes. I think at my wedding my bride and I are going to skip the cake part, don the gloves, and go three two-minute rounds instead. Why hide the violence under the guise of smiles and tradition? Get it out in the open and get it over with.

Speaking of tradition, next comes the throwing of the bouquet and the removal of the garter. These are used historically to determine who gets married next and how much good luck the newly happy couple is going to experience. This tradition always boggled me, because the only one experiencing luck is the guy who caught the garter and now has his hand up some stranger's dress. *That* is luck.

Following that ritual comes the "chicken dance" and the "hokey-pokey," both of which require bad polka music and way more coordination than is possessed by a room full of sober Italians, never mind my family. (Author's note: I have not seen a room full of sober Italians since the last time the Gotti trials were televised.) Finally there is the dance-with-the-bride-for-a-dollar ritual, where the bride sells dances with herself for money. Enjoy the dance, and be sure to pay up before cousins Vinny and Rocco, in the friendliest family sort of way, break your thumbs.

Finally, it is time to leave. Before we go, in order to be polite and also to ensure attendance at my own wedding, I must say good bye to all my relatives. They immediately begin asking when I am planning to get married, so that a date may be set and enough alcohol ordered in advance. The only thing louder than intoxicated Italians happily drinking is intoxicated Italians *no longer* happily drinking.

Friendly Skies, My Butt!

This is one of the longer ones. I remember being particularly pessimistic during one flight, because it had already been cancelled or delayed three times. When I returned, I put pen to paper to vent, and here is the result.

❦   ❦   ❦

So far in my young adult life I have done quite a bit of traveling by airplane, and therefore feel exceptionally qualified to make the following statement. *The American air travel industry is only slightly more efficient than the Russian government.* I do, of course, have several pieces of evidence to support this statement, and plan to present my argument in a logical, mature manner. If that doesn't work, I'll whine, lie, libel, and show nude photographs (it works for CNN).

It truly amazes me some of the things to which the airlines subject the average American traveler. From check-in to baggage claim, it is one huge circus, only I'm on the tightrope at 30,000 feet.

Before we even get off the ground, there is check-in. This is where we approach a counter behind which sits Princess Perma-Smile, who is way too polite to be human. She takes your ticket and your bags and punches some computer keys. Still not dimming that dazzling smile, she attaches cryptically encoded tags to your bags. Through countless hours of scientific study and exhaustive fieldwork, I have determined that these tags tell the baggage people exactly which city *not* to send your bags too. I have personally by air visited 17 major U.S. cities. My luggage has visited 32, plus two not-very-major cities, a small island nation, and Afghanistan. Princess Perma-Smile neglects to tell you that you have a better chance of scoring with a supermodel and winning the lottery (in that order) than you do of seeing your luggage at your destination.

She does not neglect to tell you that your particular flight may be over-booked, and unless you give her a cash bribe you may lose your seat. Don't worry though, the next flight leaves in just six days.

After check-in, you proceed to your departure gate, which is defined as the one farthest from wherever you are, via the security station. The security station is usually manned by old and/or overweight people who could not even with a great deal of effort stop a determined eight-year-old, much less a terror-ist. You place your carry-on items on the conveyer belt and step through the metal detector. *Beep.* You go through again, after checking to make sure you have removed all coins, keys, car motors, etc. from your person. *Beep.* You go through again, and get beeped again. After about six repetitions of this, you give up and lie that you have a metal plate in your head just so Gramps lets you by. You pick up your bag off the x-ray machine, noting that the x-ray tech is wearing a tie that looks a lot like the one you packed in your carry-on. Suffi-ciently frustrated you begin searching for your gate.

There are several different consecutive numbering systems which have been developed by mankind, and none of them are used by the airports. Gate 6 has just as much chance of being next to gate 73 as it does to gate 7. Probably more, actually. Gate numbers are also changed periodically, so that frequent flyers that are obviously being punished by God don't become too comfortable and actually begin arriving at the gate *before* the plane boards.

As you search for your departure gate you pass what appears to be the same news stand and snack bar 17 times. None of them offer a soda for less than $4, and dinner for two can cost as much as your plane ticket.

Having arrived at your gate, you notice that everything is assembled for a successful flight. There are passengers, more smiling flight attendants, a drunken, smelly man wearing upside-down pilot's wings, loud children, and … *where's the plane?* Congratulations. You have been chosen by the fates to take part in another famous air-travel tradition—the delay. You will now sit at the gate for two and a half hours while the ever-smiling flight attendant gives you fifteen minute updates on why your plane is not there. "Ladies and gentle-men we regret to inform you that flight 666 has been delayed because the pilot has no idea how to land."

Once on board the aircraft, you are subject to Newton's 17th minor law of physics, which states that the sum of the weights of the passengers in one row of airline seats must equal that of a small armored vehicle. As I only weigh about 190 pounds, you can imagine what the guy seated next to me usually looks like—a cross between Jumbo the circus elephant and Dom Delouise. A corollary to this theorem states that you will never sit next to an attractive woman who is even remotely interested in talking to you.

Next begins the safety brief. This portion of the flight is obviously provided for sheer entertainment value, as none of the safety procedures have the slightest chance in Hell of saving your life if the plane suddenly decides to stop flying at 29,000 feet. It is amusing to watch, though. The flight attendants smile beamingly as they explain what will happen "if there is a sudden loss of cabin pressure," how the little mask will drop and we can all breath normally. Right. They neglect to tell you that while the cute little mask is dropping from the ceiling, the laws of physics (major ones, this time) will be trying to blow the entire contents of the aircraft, smiling flight attendants included, through a hole about the size of a quarter. At that point, I *will* demand a refund.

After we take off, the smiling flight attendants come through the cabin with the "complimentary beverage service." This involves giving each passenger a cup full of ice and two sips of the beverage of their choice. By the time the cart gets to me, the only choices left are diet pineapple soda or clam juice. I also get a bag of exactly 3.5 peanuts.

This is usually when the "Fasten Seat Belts" sign is turned off, so that Dom the elephant can stand up and eclipse any light in the cabin. The pilot wakes up long enough to decide that *now* would be a good time to bank the aircraft, sending Dom on a collision course for my lap. As the pilot banks the other way, the person seated on the other side of me decides that *now* would be a good time to get airsick, but does *not* decide that *now* would be a good time to go for the air sickness bag. The baby in front of me decides that *now* would be a good time to start screaming. This is when I usually decide that *now* would be a good time to look into Amtrak.

Just when things are starting to resemble something bordering on an acceptable situation, it is time to land. This involves the pilot pointing the nose of the plane at the ground while simultaneously standing the plane on its wingtip. As the plane prepares for landing, the attendants make one last pass to collect any trash remaining, brutally clubbing those who refuse to relinquish their last sip of complimentary beverage.

Upon touch down, the flight attendants always remind the passengers not to unfasten seat belts until the plane has stopped moving, and the passengers always ignore them. I always find it amusing to watch the people as they leap to be the first to open the overhead compartment. These compartments are usually marked with the warning, "Caution, objects will shift during flight and probably kill you even if you are careful. We, the airline, are both sorry and completely not responsible for this." The passengers, in their collective wisdom, ignore this warning as well, and I cannot help but laugh at the poor fellow who inevitably opens up the compartment only to be buried in an avalanche of carry-on luggage.

As you disembark, the last gauntlet you must survive is the baggage claim. Good luck. First you have to find the baggage carousel that may some time in the near future (like the following Tuesday) carry luggage from your flight. Upon finding it, you must wait for your bag to be delicately placed by the baggage personnel upon the carousel. Unfortunately, the baggage personnel's idea of "delicately placed" does not exactly match anything close to the real definition. It does, however, very much match the definition of "drop-kicked."

As the bags progress around the carousel, people begin to take collect them, after first checking to make sure that they at least resemble their own, meaning they have a handle and are full of clothes. Nerves frayed from the excruciating flight finally snap, and violence often erupts. At this point I grab the nearest two bags and make a break for it, fervently praying that the person whose luggage I grabbed has better taste than I do, which according to my mother is not hard.

Personally, I think John Madden has the right idea. He buses everywhere he goes, so as not to deal with the hassle of flying. Think about it. It might take a little more time, but it is cheaper, the food is better, there are no Princess Perma-Smiles to be seen, and best of all, there is very little chance of the bus impacting the earth at over three hundred miles per hour. Unless my ex-girlfriend is driving, in which case all bets are off.

Why It's Cool to Have Sex on a Zamboni

This is a scary glimpse into the way my mind sometimes works. To be honest, my actual experiences are about 180 degrees off from what's written, but one of the reasons I write is so that I can be someone else every once in a while.

❦　　　　❦　　　　❦

Warning: Those of you ready to read a mature, intelligent, well-written essay, put this down now. This is another installment in the "Bachelor guys can do some really dumb stuff that is still pretty cool," set of lectures.

Ladies, have you ever been with a group of your friends in some particularly interesting place? Someplace like a museum, or a factory, or a historical landmark? If you have, and there were cool bachelor-type guys there, you might have noticed that they appeared lost in thought. (Actually, if it was something non-cool, like an art museum, they probably just appeared lost.) You might question aloud to your friends, "I wonder what they are thinking?" Well, today is your lucky day, because I am going to explain exactly what is running through those cool bachelor minds of those cool bachelor guys.

While you are sitting there admiring the beauty or historical significance or interior decoration or whatever of the place you happen to be, the guys, almost in unison, are thinking, "Dude, I wonder if anyone has ever *done it* up here?" Now, I have already established in more than one Pulitzer-losing essay that men pretty much think about sex from the age of thirteen until they get married, so the fact that sex enters into the equation shouldn't be too much of a surprise. But at times like this the focus actually becomes narrower. It shifts from just thinking about having sex to thinking about having sex at whatever particular unusual and supposedly significant place they happen to be.

Usually these places would normally generate as much romantic feeling as a pair of snow tires on Valentine's Day, but to the cool guy mentality, they are very stimulating. It might have something to do with dominating their environment. Most likely, it has something to do with bragging rights. There is no quicker way for a bachelor to rocket himself into the spotlight amongst his friends than to do the deed in a totally irrational and usually slightly dangerous place.

This kind of thinking has led me into perfectly rational discussions on why it would be cool to have sexual intercourse on a zamboni. For those of you who do not understand "zamboni," it is that small tractor-like vehicle which smoothes the ice out at an ice rink between periods of a hockey game. For those of you who do not understand "sexual intercourse," you should probably just roll over and die.

Typical cool guy get-togethers usually result in conversations resembling the following:

COOL GUY #1 (smirking): Guys, I did it last night.

COOL GUY #2: Yeah, well I did it on railroad tracks.

TOKEN GEEK: Guys, what's "it?"

#1: Well, we were on top of a moving train!

#2: Yeah, well then we did it again in a cement mixer!

GEEK: Did WHAT?

At this point, the conversation degenerates into each guy trying to outdo the other and alternating turns beating up the geek. Finally one guy says he did it upside down over a vat of molten metal in the middle of a snowstorm at three in the morning on the twenty-ninth of February beneath the American Flag, whereas his buddy says, "Well, who hasn't?" And the two split off to immediately find more interesting, more cool, more dangerous places to have sex so they can embellish the story to their friends.

Cool bachelor guys will have sex *anywhere*: indoors, outdoors, theaters, national monuments, or wherever. Basically, the weirder it is, the more beers we win, especially if we can prove it. That part is usually pretty difficult and often involves bribery.

I have to go now. I am meeting someone on the back of a moving snow-plow.

The Most Memorable Wedding in the World

Without a doubt, this is the most memorable wedding I have ever been to. I may even remember this one long after I have forgotten my own wedding.

❖　　　❖　　　❖

I have been to a lot of weddings. I mean *a lot*. I have *twenty-nine* first cousins, and many of them have been married more than once. In addition, several of my friends found it necessary to get married approximately twenty minutes after we graduated college, and I was in/around/immersed in quite a few of those.

Most of them all blur together. There's always a bride, a groom, cake, and me without a date. But one wedding will stand out above all the rest forever and ever. Even if I go to a transvestite wedding in the belly of a whale at the stroke of midnight on New Year's Eve, this one particular wedding will still beat it out for the all time most memorable wedding ever.

It started off ordinarily enough. It was a military wedding, and we were all dressed appropriately. That's worth mentioning, because one time I went to wedding and forgot my uniform pants. The part of the groom was played by my friend Noel. The part of the bride was played by Amy "the Mainer," who was and still is a lovely woman. Indeed her only flaw was wanting to marry Noel. Michael and I were groomsmen, along with a few others who aren't really relevant to the story. The part of the ring bearer was played by some small child whose name I can't remember.

The wedding was at the US Naval Academy Chapel, in Annapolis, Maryland, in July. Now, those of you not familiar with Annapolis in July, picture the interior of a furnace in Hell, and turn it up a few degrees. Now add 101% humidity, and there you have it. Having all been experienced with Annapolis summers, you would think we would have prepared for this, but we didn't.

Because so many of Noel's friends weren't coming in until the day before the wedding, Noel elected to have his bachelor party the night before the festive event. Noel has always been Irish (since he was born, actually) and was always proud of his ability to consume mass quantities of alcohol without so much as a missed step, so he didn't think there would be much of a problem.

Unfortunately, Noel didn't realize how popular he was, and how many people wanted to buy him a drink to celebrate his good fortune. This list included me, but that was more of a payback because Noel bought me my first shot on my 21st birthday. As a result, on the particular evening of his bachelor party, he consumed more alcohol than some *counties* in Ireland.

The following morning, that of the blessed union, Noel wasn't feeling so great. Closer to the truth, he was barely *alive.* As it was a little late to postpone things, he wisely decided to go through with the ceremony, and drank some water and took some aspirin in hopes of staving off the hangover that was beginning to caterwaul in his brain.

Because I had left the bachelor party a little earlier than Noel, I wasn't aware of just how much trouble he was in. I showed up showered, shaved, and ready to do my groomsman duties. Noel showed up looking like the wrong side of death.

The first part of the ceremony actually went pretty well, with nothing unusual to report. Noel was able to get to the altar without falling down, and so was the bride, and so were the groomsmen and bridesmaids, so everything was going according to plan. The ceremony proceeded, and actually everything was pretty tame until the part of the ceremony right before the vows. The particular ceremony the happy couple had chosen involved kneeling before the priest for that part of the ceremony. The couple kneeled on little kneelers, with their backs toward the congregation, facing the priest. As they were kneeling dutifully on the kneelers, I looked at Noel and he seemed a little pale, but otherwise OK. Then he put his head in his hands, like he was getting very emotional.

I was touched by this thought for a full second and a half before reality came shooting through. I then remembered that I had known Noel for several years, and not once did I ever remember him displaying *any* kind of emotion. Just as the bells went off in my head that something was wrong, Noel picked his head up, his eyes rolled to the back of his head, and he started a nosedive for the floor.

Time slowed dramatically in the next few moments. I shouted (well, sort of, because we were in church) to Mike to get to Noel before Noel got to the floor. Mike almost killed the ring bearer trying to get past him and out of the pew. I took the more direct route, over the rail, but got hung up and Mike still got there first. Noel was just about to hit the floor when Mike grabbed him by the back of his uniform, hoping to keep Noel and his best white uniform off the floor.

Most military uniforms, in order to be as uncomfortable as possible, involve some sort of tucking the shirt into the pants, and had Noel been wearing any of those, there would be no more to this story. As it turns out, we were all wearing our dress whites, which is a rare *untucked* uniform, so when Mike grabbed the back of Noel's shirt, he merely pulled it up as Noel's now limp body continued heading for the marble floor. We didn't know this at the time, but Noel had lost a little weight, so his pants were a little loose, and as Mike pulled up the tunic, Noel half-mooned the congregation.

We took a time out from the ceremony to revive Noel and his mother, who just about fainted at the sight of Noel's backside on what should have been the holiest day of his life. The snickers died down, and eventually we got through the rest of the ceremony without incident.

Perhaps the most remarkable thing of all was that Amy actually went through with the whole thing. I went up to her at the reception to comment on that very fact, but on the way stumbled across Noel, who looked much better, and offered me a beer. Obviously everything was back to normal.

They are still together and happily married. I am still without dates most of the time, but also happily. We still get together and drink, and almost *every time* we do, we tell this story.

How can a whale top *that*?

Some Assembly Required

This was written about thirty-three seconds after I finished furnishing my very first apartment. What a nightmare. I am now more afraid of those three words "Some assembly required" than I am of "I love you."

❦   ❦   ❦

My shirt is ripped. My thumb is swollen. My arm is scratched, and my feet hurt. My living and dining rooms should be declared disaster areas (not that the federal aid would even *begin* to get me out of debt), and it is physically impossible to get into (or out of) my apartment. There are numerous holes in the walls. The paint is scratched, the trim is chipped, and my nerves are shot. A bomb? A mother in-law? Good guesses, as both are truly frightening, destructive forces, but no.

The truth is, I actually brought this torment upon myself, and at no small expense, either. After I moved into my "new" apartment ("Not yet condemned" is a more accurate description), I realized that my furniture collection consisted of three milk crates and a couple of apple boxes. This didn't faze me much, but then the local dairy farm repossessed the milk crates (they are serious about that "penalty for illegal use" stuff), and I came to the realization that maybe I should go buy some furniture. My latest girlfriend's refusal to eat off the floor also had something to do with it, but then again she was known to have ridiculously high standards.

I began my furniture hunting in one of those stores that offers "quality furniture at reasonable prices," taking my usual cool-guy approach to shopping, defined as spending as little money as possible and not asking *any* salesperson for help, unless she's cute. This is where the problems started.

These stores sell furniture that you need to put together on your own. I knew this, and having an engineering degree, and of course being a man, I was quite confident that I could handle the challenge. A few screws, a couple of nuts, no problem. Right? I mean, the stuff all looked so good in the store, after it was all put together. How hard could it be?

Well, I soon found out. After I made my rather extensive purchases, the furniture was delivered in only seven short weeks, and it was time to assemble. I of course thought I was ready, but later, it became blatantly obvious that I was no more ready to assemble this furniture then I was ready to go to the moon. All of the boxes, including the ones which I hoped contained my couch, looked exactly the same. All of the labels were I am sure very descriptive, except that the ones which hadn't fallen off were written in Swedish. As were the three-hundred plus pages of un-illustrated instructions I found when I, in my typical organizational fashion, ripped open all twelve boxes at once and spilled their contents onto the floor of what I hoped would eventually be my living room. My very noticeably very absent money, which was supposed to have been turned into beautiful, quality furniture, now resembled a cross between giant Lincoln logs and the erector set from Hell. My evening would not improve.

About halfway through the evolution, I came to the conclusion that the store must use MIT engineering gods to put their floor models together, because there is absolutely no way on Earth that mere mortals with lowly baccalaureate degrees could accomplish this. I was either doing something wrong, or else my particular items were supposed to look like they were designed by a werewolf on a bad acid trip. I was well on my way to convincing myself that it was the latter, until my girlfriend burst my bubble (her favorite hobby). "You couldn't put two and two together," was how she put it.

Still, I am convinced that at least some of the pieces were missing. For example, apparently, all the right angles come in one box, which the delivery men must have lost, because there is none evident in any of my furniture. Also, all of my chairs, which *should*, in theory, at least resemble each other, do, in actuality, resemble pieces of modern art.

As with all nightmares, this finally ended, finding me disheveled, in a foul mood, bleeding in places, unhappy, and broke. It was a lot like most of my dates, actually.

I am planning on eating out a lot, primarily because the table can only very generously be called a horizontal surface. I also don't have many plans to entertain, unless I declare my apartment an art gallery. My girlfriend has promised to make me sleep on the couch, as soon as either of us finds it.

I miss my milk crates.

Barbie for the 21st Century

I'm pretty sure no one wants to know where my mind was on this one ...

❦   ❦   ❦

Today I saw two commercials that really bothered me. They were both for new "Barbie" products. The first one was for Barbie's kid sister; Binky, I think. She is a little darling of a toddler who apparently has learned to bleach her hair at a really young age. I am really curious as to how Barbie, who is like thirty something years old, all of a sudden has a kid sister. Her mother must be incredibly fertile, especially considering that if she is anything like Barbie, she is made of plastic and is "anatomically deficient." More on that later.

The second commercial was for "Flying Hero Barbie." Are the people at Barbie Headquarters that out of ideas that they have to resort to this? There are quite a few realistic possibilities that they missed. In the interest of public enlightenment, and perhaps suing and securing my share of the royalties, I will now publish some of my own suggestions. Hold your applause until the end.

First up is "Biker-Bitch Barbie." The hip southern California blonde trades in her Cabriolet for a Harley, and her chic uptown clothes for a leather jacket and some kickin' blue jeans. A talking version might make smart remarks and really loud gum cracking sounds, or she might just flip you off.

A variation on the leather theme is "Dominatrix Barbie." She comes complete with a whip, handcuffs, and chains. These accentuate her black leather bra and panties combination, as well as her thigh-high spiked heel leather boots. The talking version shouts encouraging things like "Lick my boots, worm!" and "On your knees, vermin!" Think of the many happy and exciting adventures she and "CEO Ken" could have!

"Streetwalker Barbie" is another one that I think would be a big hit with the kiddies. A short, tight, sequined dress, more thigh-boots, too much hair and lots of lipstick are all that is necessary for this product. The talking version says, in a husky voice, "Hey, want a date, big boy?" and other such things ("$250 dollars a night straight, an extra $50 for anything kinky.")

Here's one that I am sure Barbie's buddy Ken would love to see. How about "Anatomically Correct Barbie?" All we ever see is Ken bending over backwards to be a perfect gentleman to Barbie, but if and when he does finally hook up (that's a big IF, too, considering he's been trying since the sixties), he's only going to get half the package. I can just hear his surprise. "All that work, for *this*?" I feel like shouting to him "Hey Ken, give it up. She's got no ..." but instead, I sent this request to Barbie Headquarters:

Dear Barbie People,

Today's youth should not be sheltered from the natural wonders of the bleach-blonde's body. As evidence of what happens when you make a cake but forget the icing, I offer myself, who is actually more passionate about whether a rubber doll has nipples than he has ever been about ninety percent of his relationships. Please work on it.

Sincere, honest, and to the point.

Actually, I probably shouldn't upset the Barbie people, as my only hope for getting a date in the next decade lies in their as yet unmarketed "Inflatable Barbie" program. Hurry up, guys, I'm getting really lonely.

Mondays Suck

To be honest, there really is no point to the following beyond "Mondays suck."

❋　　　　❋　　　　❋

Will somebody please tell me what in the world is up with Monday? I don't know about you guys, but I am quite convinced that Monday is out to get me, and I for one am scared.

Nothing good ever happens on Monday. Nothing. If something ever remotely non-negative happens on Monday, something else to counteract it is sure to happen before Tuesday rolls around. If I find fifty cents on the street that morning, sure as Hell I'll get a speeding ticket that afternoon.

Let me describe a typical Monday for you. My alarm fails to go off due to a power outage. I am therefore late as I stumble in to take a cold shower (hot water also a casualty of the power outage) and pour sour milk (third casualty) on my stale cereal. As I rush out the door forgetting my wallet and my lunch I trip and fall down the stairs. It being Monday, I narrowly miss the large woman at the bottom of the stairway and instead land on her pet porcupine. The pain clears my head instantly, and I remember that I left my keys in my apartment, which is now, of course, locked.

I finally get myself back into what I think is my apartment, but not before falling off the fire escape twice. I then get arrested for breaking into what is actually my neighbor's place. The cops leave just as I realize that my car battery is dead and I need a jump. Can't pop the clutch because the tire is flat, and I *still* haven't realized that I have forgotten my wallet and my lunch.

I get to work around noon only to get jumped by the boss for being late. My computer is dead, the coffee pot is broken, the air conditioner has dripped condensation onto the report I finished at 7:00 PM on Friday, I have apparently lost my house keys, and my chair is missing. There are two messages on my voice mail. The first is from my girlfriend telling me we are no longer "right for each other." The second is from my bank. Apparently my now ex-girlfriend and I are no longer "right for each other" because she took all my money and went to Brazil with my best friend. I *still* haven't realized I have no wallet and no lunch.

Finally, someone returns my chair, but I don't notice the coffee stain until I sit in it—wearing white. All the cursing and swearing makes me hungry, and that is—*too bad*, because my lunch is rotting on the couch while my wallet (and my TV and my VCR and my stereo) is being stolen by that same honest individual who found my lost house keys.

My buddy gives me half a sandwich, which I immediately have an allergic reaction to. The ambulance crashes on the way to the hospital, and once I get there the doctor almost confuses me with the guy that needs an emergency orchiectomy, which is another name for testicle removal, which is another name for neutering.

I get home from the hospital just in time to go bed (on the floor, as my bed was stolen). Words cannot describe how happy I am that it will soon be Tuesday.

On the other, I am now free to begin dreading next Monday.

Aliens Raised my Brother

Anyone who has had both the privilege and the curse of being the oldest child knows exactly what I am talking about below. I have since learned that my parents actually allowed my less than 21-year-old brother to have a keg party, and also paid for the keg.

❦   ❦   ❦

My younger brother is not being raised by the same parents that raised me. Yes, they look like the people who raised me, and they do live in the house where I grew up, but I swear there are times when I have no idea who these people are. If it comes out later that my parents were abducted by aliens and replaced with clones, I really wouldn't have that much trouble believing it (I would however raise questions about the intelligence of a species which kidnaps suburbanites such as my parents).

I am the oldest, defined as "he who got here first," and looked upon my childhood as a time to happily learn the lessons of love and life from my parents. They, on the other hand, looked at it as an experiment. I think their attitude was, "Well, if we screw this one up, we can always make more. We're young." As I did not turn out to be a raging psychopath or a cross-dressing talk show host, I guess in the end they did a good job.

Seizing upon their experience, my parents eagerly tried to conceive another child, while I eagerly tried to conceive a way to get them to get a puppy instead. They won, and gave me a little sister, whom, for the record, I did try to return. She is the middle child, defined as "she who hated the oldest and the youngest from infancy to adulthood," and it was her responsibility to grow up and conform to all the stereotypes that people who never have children dream up for middle children. My parents applied basically the same rules to her as they did to me, and in the end she turned out OK too.

Then came my brother, the youngest, defined as "he who is allowed to get away with things that would have gotten the first two children beaten with a snow shovel". It is his job to be spoiled rotten and get away with just about anything. He's very good at it, too.

As an example, both my sister and I had to eat lima beans. We both hated lima beans. When I say "hated" I am talking about the same type of hate that cats feel toward water, or Americans feel towards the IRS. *That* kind of hate. We were not allowed to leave the table until we ate all our lima beans, and as a result of that I once missed two and a half weeks of school. I spent that entire time at the kitchen table trying to choke down three lousy beans. According to my father, I was "building character." My brother not only is allowed to leave the table before he finishes his lima beans, but he can substitute any vegetable he wants, like pizza. My brother's definition of a vegetable also includes corn dogs and peanut butter. He doesn't even have to come to the table if he doesn't want to. He can eat off the floor in his room, and my parents just "overlook" it.

Dating is an even better example. When I was in eighth grade, I wanted to take this sweet young thing to the movies. She was everything I could want in a date, which at thirteen meant she wore a bra and was alive, so I asked my parents for permission to ask her out.

Hoooooleeeey Cow. My parents were so beside themselves we had to set extra places at dinner. Their little *darling* wanted to ask some floozy on a *date*?

"Mom, she's not a floozy," I argued.

"Does she wear a bra?" I nodded emphatically, as I had researched the subject intently. "Then she's a floozy." Mom was known not to think all that clearly in times of crisis.

There followed for the next two weeks one of the most agonizing periods of my childhood. All I wanted was a yes or no answer and maybe a ride and instead I got speeches and questions and audio-visual presentations with a level of detail not seen by the Joint Chiefs of Staff. Finally, after much deliberation, and promises that I would not get married before I at least finished the ninth grade, my parents decided it would be acceptable to let me ask the object of my desires to a movie. I did, and learned that afternoon that the only desire she had toward me was to have her older brother run over me with his car. I was crushed (almost literally), and would have to wait some time (seven years, three months, two weeks, and four days) until my first date.

My brother, on the other hand, went on his first date when he was in sixth grade, was given new clothes, money, and the keys to the car for the evening. Now, that's fair. Then my parents wonder why I play fun games like "Catch the Javelin" with him when I come home.

He comes and goes as he pleases, as long as he does his chores. His chores are defined as taking the trash from the kitchen to the door leading to the garage, and actually closing the front door behind him. For this, he earns an allowance of $37.50 a week, tax-free. Not to sound bitter, but when I was his age, my chores broke *Chinese* child labor laws, and my annual allowance was slightly less than the change that can be found in the cushions of the couch you are seated on.

My siblings and I each love our parents dearly. My sister and I for the strong, steady discipline and support they provided for us in our formative years. My brother because he has more privileges and less responsibility than Britain's royal family.

That's OK, though. He loans me a few bucks every so often.

Personal Ads and Personal Disasters

Obviously, this one came about when the girlfriend was no longer part of the equation. I did actually try the personals, both newspaper and internet, and met some really great people. I also met some complete freaks. It was pretty much the same odds as going to a bar, except you don't come away smelling like smoke.

❋   ❋   ❋

Recently, I became single. It is not like I was actually married, but we had been living together for four months, and we fought a lot and stopped having sex (at least with each other), so that was close enough. Anyway, it was over, as evidenced by her throwing all of my stuff out of her twelfth story bedroom window, and I was once again turned loose upon the female populace.

Having been out of the singles scene for some time, I was not sure where to start. I tried the bar scene, but was somewhat less successful than Custer at the Little Big Horn and I bled more besides. I was getting pretty frustrated and pretty desperate, and began to think, "Where else can I find quality, frustrated, equally desperate people like me?"

After much thought and much more beer, it hit me. There are only two places to look. Church and the personals. The last time I went to church, the priest went into convulsions and my clothes caught fire, so that kind of narrowed it down.

I had never tried the personals. But of course I had heard wonderful things about it from about a dozen of my friends (who, now that I think about it, had exactly two dates among them in three years), and the whole idea made pretty good sense to me. Here were a whole slew of women who obviously did not have the time to meet men because according to the ads they were all doctors or lawyers or bankers. They would like nothing better than to have me call them up so we can get together and live happily ever after, or at least have lots of sex.

Imagine my pleasant surprise when I read the ads and discovered that not only were all the advertisers professional, educated, independent women, but they were all "slim, attractive, and waiting for me." This was going to be so much easier than the "meet a girl in a bar, make small talk, get slapped" scenario that I had become used to. The world was my oyster ...

OK, now comes the part of the story referred to as *The Awakening*. I would like to pass on a couple of things I learned about the personals. Pay attention people, this could save your life. First of all, even though the ads appear in that bastion of truth, the morning newspaper, the advertisers are really under no obligation to advertise the truth, or anything even closely resembling the truth. Because some women do not want to advertise that they have the physique of a rhino and are pursuing a career in fast food, they tend to get a little creative. It only took me about fourteen dates to realize this. I kept thinking things would improve. "They can't *all* have lied," I thought. I was only slightly completely wrong. Three of these fine, young, completely dishonest ladies outweighed me. The rest outweighed me *and* the car they drove up in.

And this was not free, either. The cost of answering ads was $13.78 a minute. Of course, the voice mail speaks to you in a southern drawl, so the phrase "Welcome to the personal ads. Please make a selection," takes more time than to say than Richard Nixon was in office. The bottom line is that I had to take out a loan in order to pay for the privilege of meeting dishonest overweight tollbooth attendants who had described themselves as "attractive, well rounded, government officials."

The choice between bankruptcy and dating more ultra-behemoths was surprisingly easy, so I decided not to answer any more ads. I decided to place my own ad. I took very few creative liberties, adding only three years to my age, subtracting 20 pounds off my weight, and changing "junior naval officer" to "underwear model." They lie, I lie. I said I was looking for a mature, athletic woman with whom to have dinner, and sat back and waited for the messages to come flooding in.

I would like to point out to a disappointedly large (yes, pun intended) portion of the female population that our definitions of the word "athletic" are obviously different. My definition is someone who is in shape, works out seriously, and plays several different sports. Your definition of "large enough to be a softball backstop" does most certainly *not* qualify.

There were two women who answered my ad that were not slightly completely overweight. The first one not only fell out of the ugly tree, but obviously hit *every* branch on the way down. My meeting with the second one went a bit better. We had a great time, just me and her *and her parole officer.*

That was it, the cinder block that broke this camel's back. I am obviously destined to die old and lonely, and anything I do is only going to prolong the agony. The only eligible, attractive woman who speaks to me is my ex, but I can't really write what she said.

I have placed another ad, this time being brutally honest. "Desperate white male seeks anyone without her own zip code, a record, or a face that stops traffic."

No calls yet.

Redneck Softball

As scary as it sounds, there is an awful lot of truth in the following story. Nothing in the world prepares a kid from New Jersey for his first real exposure to rednecks, and I was even more unprepared than most.

❋   ❋   ❋

Girls love athletes. It is an absolute fact that most male professional athletes do what they do solely to pick up babes. Some of the female professional athletes do to, but we won't go into that.

Taking that into consideration, and being on a particularly lengthy dry spell as far as women were concerned, I began looking for ways to introduce more athletics into my life. First, I tried golf, but got in trouble after drawing my 3-wood to duel Zorro-style with a golfer who wanted to play through. On to tennis, where I threw three rackets through four windows in two days. Racquetball reminded me too much of tennis, so that was out, and I began to wonder if I would ever again enjoy the wide world of sports.

Finally, a co-worker told me about the softball league he was in, and asked if I was interested. I jumped at the chance, and signed up without realizing what I was getting into. Two weeks later, I met my team, and have been with them for two seasons. I am now going to introduce the Benzington Beer-Swillers to you, so that you may share the bond with these fine athletes that I do.

First, there is Randy, who is both the coach and King Redneck of the local tri-county area. He is six-four, has long blond hair, and skin that is always sunburned, even in December. He drives a pick-up truck that is only slightly younger than I am, and which is primarily the color of rust. It starts and runs about two days out of seven. It does, however, have a brand new gun rack in it. At practice, he drinks a beer and smokes a pack of cigarettes, in preparation for games, when he drinks two beers and smokes two packs. I have never, in two years, under any circumstances, seen Randy without a baseball hat on. It has never come off during a game. Not due to wind, or running, or sliding, or me standing on his shoulders trying to yank it off. I think it may actually be sewn to his head. Randy is the pitcher.

He works most with the catcher, Ernie, who is one of the few non-rednecks on the team. Ernie is actually a very large Filipino. He is ideally suited to be the catcher, because when he blocks the plate, he usually also eclipses the sun.

The first baseman is Eric, who is only a partial redneck. He does drive a pickup, but doesn't know how to fish and can use all twenty-six letters of the alphabet. Because of this, he is somewhat of an outcast, and often discriminated against during team social functions, like mud rastlin'.

Second is played by either Cindy or Joannie. Cindy was high-school homecoming queen in three of her last five years in high school. Joannie just gave birth to her second child. She's seventeen. Her teeth also serve as the team bottle opener after the games. We decide who starts by having them count backward from five and see who wins. Sometimes, we have to do it a couple of times to get both of them all the way through.

I play shortstop, and as a Yankee born and raised in New Jersey, often feel the need to slap the back of my neck for twenty or thirty minutes before game time just to fit in with my redneck team mates. If I don't, they do it for me.

Chuck's got third. He is nineteen, and about to have his first child. Second, if you count the fact that his wife is sixteen. He has got a wicked arm with a *lot* of tattoos, and is on the fast track in his career. By the year 2020, he is expected to be the assistant manager of the gas station.

Billy Bob, Jo Bob, and Bobby Jo make up the outfield. They come from a close family: Jo Bob and Bobby Jo are both brother and sister and first cousins, and Billy Bob is an uncle and a husband to another member of the family. They are very generous with each other, meaning that they take turns sharing the three shoes their family owns.

At the end of every game, we celebrate our victory, or at least the fact that everyone was able to find the game, even though we always play at the same field. We do this with beer and a cook out. It is a very relaxing time, where we talk about important redneck issues, such as pick up trucks, dogs, cut off shorts, and where the fish are biting.

We are more than just a softball team. We have become a family (well, some of them already *were* family). We are short on talent, short on manners, short on teeth, but we have *lots* of character, and lots of beer. Occasionally we win, often we lose, but there is something to be said for a sport that apparently can not be legally played without alcohol.

Traveling with Mr. Chang

The following is an almost completely factual account, which after you read it should scare the bejeezus out of you regarding government practices. I changed just enough to prevent lawsuits and a reassignment to Antarctica.

❋   ❋   ❋

The government in its infinite (esimal) wisdom recently sent me on my first business trip. This in itself would have been exciting, except that the government also sent on this excursion another business trip virgin, Mr. Chang.

As a quick biological sketch of Mr. Chang, I provide the following. Mr. Chang is "chronologically challenged." This means that, technically, he is older than dirt. He is well beyond that birthday when most people stop caring about manners, their appearance, and restraining personal flatulence. He is a health food fanatic, meaning he usually eats only bean curd and brussel sprouts and is planning to live to be 100. He is also an immigrant, and has been able after several years in this country to master exactly three words of the English language. This does not keep him from being three of the five most talkative people I have ever met. He has little real communication skills, less personal warmth, and is not quite as personable as a rabid gorilla with hemorrhoids, though his personal hygiene is slightly better. Typical government logic has assigned him to customer relations.

Mr. Chang does not like to drive. The state and its life-loving citizens do not like Mr. Chang to drive either. Therefore, I had to pick Mr. Chang up and drive him to the airport. On the way, he was very opinionated concerning the problems with my generation—I think. Either that or he was discussing how to roast chicken in motor oil. That accent is a killer. I also discovered another one of my companion's little idiosyncrasies. He is an absolute master of the obvious. "Oooh, so wen yu puush da pedal down, da caw go." Yes, Mr. Chang. Upon arriving at the airport, we parked the car in satellite parking, which gets its name from the number of times you orbit the lot looking for the one space that is still open, and proceeded to the terminal. Mr. Chang tried to make conversation. "So, da shuttle gonna com fo us, o wat?" No, you fossilized vapor factory, we have to walk seventeen miles to the damn airport carrying my one bag and your seven.

At the check-in, Mr. Chang decided to take issue with the young lady behind the counter.

"So, wat yu need to see my ID? I not a tewwowist!"

"Sir, we need to check everyone's ID."

"I not a tewwowist! You tink da tewwowist have an ID dat say 'tewwowist.' I not tink so."

"No, sir, you are not a terrorist, but I need to see an ID."

"OK, hewe it is. You nice giwl. Why not you mawwied?"

"Security to the check-in counter. Security …"

I grabbed my companion and gently nudged him with an elbow to his elderly ribs toward our gate. As we move towards the gate, he alternates between stating that he is not a tewwowist and demanding that I marry the counter girl. My day would not improve.

Finally, we boarded the plane. Mr. Chang and I of course had adjacent seats (Good one, God!), so the entire trip I was treated to a dissertation on what is wrong with the government. Or how to make your own cheese; damn that accent! The only time he stopped talking was to either bother the male flight attendant, ("Eh, you not mawwied. Awe yu gay?") or burp. At this point I was praying for the wings to fall off. Plunging to a fiery death seemed to pale in comparison to listening to my cohort's ranting. What he lacked in pronunciation he more than made up for in volume. On the other hand, I could just hear him ask as we plummeted earthward, "So, we gona cwash, o wat?".

When we landed, I tried to lose my companion at the baggage claim (and the snack shop, and the newsstand, and the car rental counter) but failed miserably. We got to our vehicle, and departed for the hotel. I drove, he navigated. In four hours we had crossed the state line six times and traveled a net distance of six miles. He blamed the map, Richard Nixon, and Communism. I blamed myself for failing to come up with a believable alibi and a method of disposing of the body.

Thankfully, Mr. Chang and I had separate rooms. Separate hotels would have been better, but at this point ten minutes to myself was like heaven.

With dinner rapidly approaching, I came to the realization that I was in a strange city with absolutely nothing to do until the next morning, and the only person I knew within 500 miles I was not reasonably sure I could dine with without killing. Dinner actually went surprisingly well, as Mr. Chang was so busy shoving food into his mouth and chewing with his mouth open that he did not have time to harangue me. He did mention something about religion (or new shoes, I couldn't tell), and then thankfully dessert arrived. I managed to fake a splitting headache, probably because I had one, so that I was allowed to retire early.

The next morning I met Mr. Chang in the lobby for breakfast. I was wearing slacks and a modest shirt. He was wearing yellow plaid pants with a pink shirt, a lime green sports coat, and a fedora hat. I tried to hide, but the one thing of his that isn't going is his eyesight, and he picked me out from behind the potted fern.

Breakfast was the first thing on the agenda. Typical people enter the restaurant, sit down, peruse the menu, and order something in a reasonable amount of time. It took my esteemed cohort *19 minutes* to read the menu and decide that he didn't see anything he liked. I stated that I was having the buffet bar, and he said he wanted to go see it. I agreed to show him where it was in the desperate hope that we could have breakfast before it was time to go to dinner. Mr. Chang was not overly impressed with the breakfast bar, but on the way back to our table, he did see something that caught his eye. Unfortunately, it was on another patron's plate. While this poor man sat there trying to have his pancakes and coffee with his wife, Mr. Chang was two feet away watching him chew every bite. That was bad enough, but then he began to ask questions about the meal. "Oh, is dat good? U like dat? I doon know if I coud eat dat." The man did his best to ignore my companion, but how do you ignore an ancient artifact sitting practically in your lap while you are buttering your toast? Check, please.

Finally, Mr. Chang decided he would order the pancakes, sausage, juice and coffee special, as long as he could substitute French toast, bacon, milk, and tea. The waiter was willing to go along with anything that would get us out of his restaurant, so finally, about two o'clock in the afternoon, we finished breakfast and left.

The next day's schedule involved a breakfast buffet. Mr. Chang made four trips to the bar, but the only thing I saw him eat was half a bagel and some grapes. He did, however, appear to be gaining an incredible amount of weight right in front of my eyes. This was because he was stuffing everything he could get his greedy hands on into his pockets. He had four bagels, a box and a half of tea bags, more sugar packets than South America could possibly produce in a day, and silver service for seven, plus a serving tray. (Author's Note: Do *not* invite Mr. Chang to your house for dinner.)

The conference continued, and Mr. Chang's performance was incredibly consistent. He managed to offend at least one person in every single workshop he attended. He also managed to offend three people in the workshops *I* attended, which did not endear me to anyone. As an added bonus, he managed to reduce our hotel maid to tears by alternating between asking for towels and asking why she was not married.

Thankfully, the conference ended just before the State legislature was about to deport us. I was able to escape conversation on the plane by feigning sleep. Actually, it was more like feigning a coma. I did not *move* for four hours, held in one position not by relaxation or tired muscles but by the blind fear of the conversation which would ensue if I was detected to be awake.

He actually left me alone until right before we landed, when he woke me up to express concern that we might not find the car. I assured him that we would. He again expressed concern. "Der aw so many caws. You weally tink we can find it? I not tink so. We be wost hewe fo wong time." At that point, I was ready to tell him that if we could not find the car, I would steal someone else's just to drive him home and have this ordeal end. I held my tongue, though (with my teeth.)

We landed, and proceeded to the baggage claim. We were delayed when Mr. Chang noticed a small scratch on one of his bags, and immediately threatened the Sky cap and his entire family with death if it was not immediately repaired. The Sky cap responded by seizing both Mr. Chang's luggage and mine and throwing it in front of a shuttle bus. I intervened, grabbing Captain Ancient and dragging him with me until finally we arrived at my car. I broke the land speed record in the seven-year-old-vehicle-that-was-a-hand-me-down-from-my-parents category in order to get Mr. Chang home before I was forced to destroy him.

I have personally told the boss that I would rather be fired than travel again with Mr. Chang. The boss has personally told me that Mr. Chang and I are scheduled to travel to California for two weeks, but promised to fire me when I got back. We leave immediately.

Dating Too Close to Home

For a while, I wasn't really all that selective about who I went out with. Basically, if she would talk to me and weighed less than I did, she was the one for me. As a result, I fell into the following trap. Twice.

❀   ❀   ❀

I don't think you guys appreciate the sacrifices I make in order to provide material to my audience. I continuously search for new and exciting ways to get myself into trouble, in order that I may enlighten you and save you from horrible embarrassment and, quite possibly, jail time.

My latest screw up was getting involved with a girl who lived in my apartment complex. Guys, never, *never* do this. No matter how well it appears to be going, no matter how much fun you are having, no matter how good a cook she is, sooner or later, it will bite you in the ass. Trust me on this one, I know.

I would never, ever, even to make a publication deadline, write something that wasn't 100% factual (or at least *really* funny), and of course am going to back up my warnings with factual evidence. The reason I know what a bad idea this is because I have done it. In the interest of further educating my readers and because I am basically an idiot I have done it twice.

The basic problem is that there is never a good enough excuse not to hang out with this person. It usually goes something like this:

HER: "Are you coming over later?"

ME: "Well, I am sort of pretty beat. Can't we just pass until tomorrow?"

HER: "Oh, come on. I'm just a few doors down. Come watch TV."

ME: "Uh, well, I need to study."

HER: "Just come by when you are done."

ME: "Uh, well, actually, my, uh, kitchen is on fire."

HER: "Well, when you put it out, just come on *over*. I am only a few doors down. See you later."

ME: "Uh, sure."

The first time I ran into this problem, I was living with a buddy in Florida. I bumped into this girl in the apartment complex gym, and we started talking, and we got along, and I, very innocently, not wanting anything more than friendship (one night stand), asked her if she wanted to come over and have leftovers with me and my roommate. (Author's note: Leftovers are considered by single men to be a basic food group.) We had a great time, got along, and eventually, hooked up, which was of course all her idea. It was an incredible night of romance, after which, apparently, I was expected to call or propose or something. Now, had this been a normal situation, with a girl that lived anywhere but in the same complex as me, I would have been able to deal with it, fake my own death, and move on. However, as she lived in my apartment complex, it was a whole different ballgame. She would come home and look for my car. If she saw it, she would call and say "Oh, I saw your car, and knew you were home." If she didn't see the car, she would call anyway, and ask my roommate where I was. It took a while for me to catch on to this one. One time I parked the car in a vacant lot across the street and disguised it as an abandoned vehicle (which, for my car, involves leaving the door open) and, of course, she called. I answered the phone and had to pretend I was my twin brother just in from Albuquerque. It worked. Thankfully, she was cute, but not all that bright. The whole thing came to a crashing halt when I had her arrested on stalking charges.

OK, life continues, lesson learned. Right? Wrong. Fast forward my life to last month. Same me, different apartment, different girl, different state. I was wearing the same sweatshirt, though. This time, I wasn't looking for romance, or commitment, or even a one night stand. Specifically, I was looking for an egg. I was baking a cake, and I needed one egg, so I knocked on my neighbor's door to borrow said egg. Then she opened the door. I asked for the egg, she gave me the egg, I baked the cake. To be neighborly, and to avoid returning the egg (because I had broken it), I brought her a piece of cake. She ate the cake. She liked the cake. I went home.

Next day, she came over and wanted more cake. In trade, she would make me dinner. What she really wanted was me for dessert. Being male, I resisted her carnal charms for at least four minutes, but then I weakened.

Apparently, after I saw her again and we repeated the dessert incident, she felt that she too was entitled to a phone call or a friendly nod in the parking lot, or some other such courtesy. It took her a while to catch on that I did not necessarily agree. I think it became obvious when to avoid her I began entering and leaving my apartment by way of the balcony. I lived on the sixth floor.

This went on for about three months, until I got arrested for breaking and entering. I was returning from an evening on the town, and was somewhat intoxicated. I climbed up to the wrong balcony, in the wrong building. Anyway, the charges were dropped, but she said she couldn't continue our relationship (what relationship?) if I was a potential felon. I told her that had I known that, I would have knocked over a bank the week after we met. She is now suing me for the value of one egg, appreciated over four months, plus mental anguish. The bottom line is around $300K. We didn't part on the best of terms.

Because of these rather eye-opening experiences, I have developed some life rules to prevent these sorts of things from happening again. Specifically, I never even speak to my neighbors anymore, and when dating, never use my real name. I have moved to another apartment complex, which is the local geriatric community (I lied about my age), so I am not even tempted. Finally, I buy eggless cake mix. I'll keep you posted.

I Drink Because I Coach Youth Basketball

Despite the insanity described when I was coaching t-ball, I couldn't resist the calling to coach basketball. I should have tried harder.

✿ ✿ ✿

In my pursuit of community service, and also to get a lighter sentence, I recently began coaching a youth basketball team. As I signed up to coach, I remember being full of idealistic thoughts (or maybe it was bourbon) about how I would make a difference to my young players, and how I would inspire them to great feats upon the court, and rack up an undefeated record, and other such wonderful things. I confidently predicted that we would go 7-0, and would do better if the season were only longer.

I diligently began making plans for our first practice. I would evaluate my talent pool, and using that knowledge, would teach them the 2-1-2 zone, the pick and roll, and the fast break. I would instill a defensive mentality which would resist scoring just like every woman I have ever gone out with. Our passing would befuddle the other team, our strength intimidate them, and our defense harass them at every turn. A 7-0 season was not only possible, it was inevitable.

Ten minutes into the first practice, I realized that the talent pool was a little shallow in places, and I would have to get more basic, so we started to work on dribbling, passing, and shooting. Ten minutes after that, it finally dawned on me that the pool was empty, and that we needed to get even more basic, so we concentrated on using complete sentences when we spoke, and running without falling down. We pressed on, as the first game loomed on the horizon. I realistically changed my prediction to a more conservative 5-2.

Before we could play in the first game, the league officials had decided to further torture us with Opening Ceremonies. This took place sometime around 5:00 AM on a Saturday morning, and consisted of lining up all the teams on the gym floor, inspiring them with words spoken by three or four people who may or may not be able to pick a basketball out of a line up, and then giving them lots of cookies. That is just what you want to do with approximately 150 kids, ages 6-12; wake them up early and give them unlimited sugar.

The scheduled guest speaker for the event did not show, so they dragged Lou the Janitor out and got him to speak instead. He immediately harangued the audience about not putting gum under the bleachers, and how the rising cost of Pine Sol was the fault of those godless communists. Lou spends a little too much time sniffing the floor wax, if you know what I mean. Not that we could hear him, as the microphone wasn't working, but he sure looked good. Billy Graham would have been proud. Anyway, just as Lou was wrapping up, my assistant coach catches my attention and tells me to start looking at the competition. I do, and immediately notice that *every* team in our age group, plus two from the younger age group, is on average six inches taller than my tallest kid. From this I gathered that some of the parents got a little creative with their children's ages. This was further confirmed when I saw two kids *drive* to opening ceremonies. With the season opener one week away, the picture was looking bleak for my under-talented, under-tall group of warriors. I changed my prediction to 3-4 for the season.

We continued to practice hard for the first game. I divided the team into two squads. The first worked on shooting, passing, dribbling, and playing defense. The second worked on drooling, falling down, and fouling out in the first six minutes of each game. I had two kids who could really play, another four who were somewhat productive, and four more whom I was reasonably sure could breathe without assistance. Our practices consisted of the coaches demonstrating the drills, and the players trying very hard to do the exact opposite. In no way, shape, or form did anything they do resemble basketball. My prediction sank to 2-5. Somebody, somewhere in the league, was worse.

As much as I hoped and prayed against it, the first game rolled around. We were playing the Warriors. Their smallest kid was 5'-4", and shaved. Three of my kids showed up with their jerseys on backwards. Two more showed up without jerseys altogether. This was after three *weeks* of practice.

Halfway through the first quarter, we were down 12-0. We took three shots in that time (two of them on our own basket—my point guard got a little excited). I looked to my assistant coaches for support. One of them was in tears and the other one was cowering under the bleachers. It was not one of the finer moments in youth sports. On the spot I changed my season prediction to 0-7.

My team does deserve a lot of credit for the ingenious ways in which they created new fouls during the game. I can honestly say that until this game I had never seen a tackling foul, or a bear hugging foul, or a tying-the-opponent's-shoes-together foul. That last one was one of my brighter kids.

Eventually, we lost 44-6. We scored three times; one time by accident when my shooting guard tried to pass the ball to his father in the stands, and two shots that can only be described as "A whole lot of Hail Mary's."

Practice the next week was difficult. There is no coaching book in the world (believe me, I looked) that prepares you for what to say to your team after such a defeat. "Well, at least we didn't get shut out," just seemed woefully inadequate. I tried to be positive. "Well, you *all* didn't stink," I stammered. I also tried to concentrate on only the good points, while downplaying the negatives. It was an incredibly short speech. At this point, my predictions started to extend into next season. Actually, I was reasonably sure that I could put all 10 of my players on the court at one time and still lose.

With two games left, after we were 0-5 and had been outscored 312-21 for the season, the unbelievable happened. We *won!* Apparently, the other coach was either cursed, was sleeping with the ref's wife, or just really on God's s#$% list. *Everything* these guys did went wrong, compared with only about 94% of what we did. We won the game 6-4, in overtime, by using the ingenious strategy of throwing the ball into the air anytime we crossed half court. I think I was more excited than the kids were. I was on an emotional high for what seemed like forever. It actually lasted until our next practice, when we lost our scrimmage 27-2.

Still, having beaten the odds to win one game, I was actually looking forward to the next game, and didn't need to take tranquilizers beforehand. To celebrate our victory, and to inspire our children to even greater feats, two of the coaches wore suits and ties to the game. Eddy wore jeans and a T-shirt with no holes, but that is a huge step up for him. As the game was about to be begin, we were full of confidence.

Our confidence and our winning streak died quickly. By the end of the first quarter, we were down 18-0. By halftime, it was 32-2, and, in our great team tradition, we had scored by accident. By the end of the third quarter, it was really ugly, and midway through the fourth, the refs awarded a TKO because all my players had fouled out.

The season ended, and at the team party, it was my intention to comment on the good points of our season, and stress how we had improved and come together as a team. Unfortunately, I had been reduced to a drooling vegetable that stared into space and mumbled things like "We just missed too many lay-ups. I thought they would go in but they didn't. It's not my fault," over and over. My assistants covered for me with thoughtful, motivating words. In short, they lied. The parents gave us gifts to thank us for all of our hard work, and further thanked us for not killing any of their children, even the ones that deserved it.

My one assistant coach and I have both decided not to coach for a while. My other assistant coach has been found "not competent to make decisions," and is waiting further psychiatric evaluation. There is no real future in being a basketball coach. Even if I ever get good enough to coach in the NBA, I would still be coaching children, only this time, they would be big enough to beat me up.

Office Folders
(a new way to torment your
employees)

At my first real job, the deputy was completely incompetent when it came to communication. It was like dealing with a 200Gb hard drive on a 286 MHz computer. You knew the info was there, but it was just too painful an experience to get to it. We knew she was horrible at communicating, and she was so bad she even realized it, and set forth one week to change forever her reputation as a poor office communicator. Her efforts inspired the following.

❦   ❦   ❦

Recently, there have been some changes in the way things are done around my office. We used to have two types of correspondence folders. A green folder meant routine stuff; schedules, instructions for the staff, memos from management, Victoria's Secret catalogs, that type of thing. Red folders meant some sort of action was required, like a response letter or arranging to have someone beaten up. All in all, a pretty simple system. It was easy to learn, simple to use, and occasionally, despite management's best efforts, we got things done.

Now the powers that be (stupid), sensing that the employees were actually beginning to finish things before 6 PM on Friday, decided to change the system so as to keep morale in the toilet. They also decided that maybe they should add a few folders, just in case there was a situation that didn't quite fit into the existing system. Now we have green folders for routine correspondence, red folders for important stuff, blue folders for really important stuff (like naked pictures of the boss's wife), and purple folders for correspondence from the Pope (but those are rare).

I think management stopped too soon. There are at least four people in the office who are not totally fed up and/or confused with the new system. Therefore, in the interest of TQL (a management buzzword, which stands for Tolerating Queers and Lesbians), I have written a memo to be circulated. In a green folder, of course.

"The following will be the new color code for all correspondence, effective immediately. Failure to master this new system will result in death by firing squad."

Green—still denotes routine correspondence.

Red—correspondence from the office manager.

Red, With Green Stripes—denotes Christmas correspondence.

Blue—correspondence from the regional manager

Blue, With A Yellow Crown—correspondence from the queen

Red, With White Stripes And A Blue Field—correspondence from the President

Red, With A Pitchfork—correspondence from Satan, or the deputy director

Red, With A Yellow Star, And Bursting At The Seams—correspondence concerning China

Red, White, And Green—correspondence concerning Italy

Purple—still denotes correspondence from the Pope

White, With A Red Cross—correspondence from the company medical staff

See Through—correspondence dealing with lingerie

Pink—correspondence dealing with homosexual issues

Two Pink Folders, Both Neat, And A Little Masculine—memos dealing with the secretary and her female friend from accounting.

Orange—correspondence concerning Florida

White, With A Red Maple Leaf—correspondence concerning Canada

Brown—memos full of crap

Black—correspondence dealing with Armageddon

Black, With White Stripes—correspondence dealing with zebras

Black, With Orange Border—correspondence dealing with Halloween

Black, With Skull And Crossbones—correspondence dealing with the cafeteria

Green, Soaked With Beer—correspondence dealing with St. Patrick's Day

White, Rough Around The Edges, Soaked With Beer—memos dealing with our maintenance man

Yellow, Found On Top Of Above Folder In A Dark Room—memos dealing with the boss's daughter.

Invisible—deals with pay raises, increased benefits, and holidays

This new system should cover every possible scenario we could run into in my office. If it doesn't, management will most likely blame us as a group, or me, personally, via memo, in a green folder.

The Appliance Strikes Back

I forget what inspired this one. I think my toaster broke. Whatever it was, it wasn't anywhere near what's described below. But if you paid money to read about a broken toaster, you would probably be pretty mad.

❋   ❋   ❋

There is a full-scale appliance revolution going on in my apartment.

It started when just recently I bought a new computer. I had to, because I also just recently became single, and all of a sudden had nothing in my life to baffle me, make me feel inadequate, or make strange noises. I got *the* machine, too. It has absolutely everything, or at least that is what the salesman explained to me as he took all of my money away. Sixteen rams that byte and megahertzes and bauds and hard driving and a whole bunch of other words that I don't begin to understand. That doesn't stop me from using them to try and pick up women, though. "Hey babe, want to come home and see my hard drive." *Smack!*

Now I am about as experienced with computers as I am with women, so realize that I don't have a whole lot to work with here. But still, you would think I should have been able to perform the most rudimentary functions, like turning the damn thing on, without incident. *Not.* Things actually started off OK. At first, it was just like a new pet; all cute and cuddly and really easy to get along with, until it realized that you couldn't send it back. Then it started being less than cooperative. Actually, it started being downright insulting.

Every time I tried to get it to do something, it would make this obscene burping noise, and a message screen would pop up explaining that I must be the children of immigrant pig farmers for trying to tell it to actually do something. It was like an electronic mother-in-law.

I tried to make it print. *Burp.* "Printer not connected, you moron." I tried to copy files. *Burp.* "Disk is still write-protected, Neanderthal." I tried to back up my hard drive. *Burp.* "Get real, stupid."

When I finally did get it to print, the first thing I did was write a letter to my ex asking for forgiveness and would she reconsider. I happened to be in a hurry, and didn't proof read my letter all that carefully (or at all). I later found out, via a brick through my window, that my machine had taken a few "liberties" in my letter. For example, where I had written, "My love for you knows no bounds," the computer had printed "Your feet stink, your toes are hairy, you have lizard's breath, and I have seen better legs on a piano." After further consideration, it was definitely more honest than my original letter, but that doesn't replace my window.

My high tech TV/VCR combo unit decided that if it was OK for the computer to revolt, than it might as well get in on the act too. It decided for absolutely no reason to stop working right in the middle of the World Series. Then it decided to only get gospel stations. Then it decided to get only *Spanish* gospel stations. Of course, boy-genius that I am, I asked myself "Can things get any worse?"

Of course they can, and they did. The clock radio now only wakes me up in the middle of the night or on Saturday mornings, by imitating some sort of nuclear device. The fire alarm helps, too. When I actually need to get up, it decides to imitate a mime. The toaster oven oscillates between incinerating my toast and melting it. The microwave, not to be outdone, refuses to cook anything without making it explode. The refrigerator won't keep food cold, the oven won't make it hot, and the thermostat has decided to heat the bedroom to five degrees shy of hell, screeching like a banshee in the process.

The answering machine has played havoc on what social life I did have. It conveniently forgets any message left by a person who actually wanted to talk to me. It does, however, remember any message from a wrong number or phone solicitor or crackpot or ex-girlfriend who dials my number. Not only does it remember them, it actually refuses to allow me to delete them, and often plays them randomly at three-thirty in the morning.

The washer has turned all of my clothes to one shade of brown. Not that it matters, as the dryer has shrunk all of my clothes so that only an overweight Barbie can wear them. (*You* try wearing boxer shorts 21 sizes too small.) The hot water heater is being the kindest. It doesn't do anything but go *klink* once every eight seconds. At least, I think it is eight seconds. I have six clocks, and they have formed a small alliance with the single goal of not agreeing on anything, ever. One of them runs backwards.

I decided to use my old trusty college calculator to determine how much it would cost to replace all my rebel appliances. Regardless of whatever operation I tried and whatever numbers I used, the answer was always 17 and $\frac{1}{2}\pi$ dollars and -6 cents. *Et tu, Brute?*

My one hope at retaliation lay in not paying the electric bill. My plot was foiled when the computer logged me on to the Information Superhighway, where I am known as "Roadkill," and paid my electric bill for the next 47 months. This, coupled with some other really lovely computer-controlled investments, such as $2000 to the "Unabomber for President" fund, have left me with approximately $12.37 until the year 2012. That's before taxes.

I have decided to call a meeting and ask for terms of surrender, before things get really violent and the mixer and electric knife come after me.

Pass. Dribble. Fall Down.

Last coaching story. I promise.

❦   ❦   ❦

First, I coached baseball. 0-16 record, and my star player almost got a hit. Then, I coached basketball. We almost won a game by forfeit, but then their point guard and their water boy showed up, and the two of them beat us 67-2. While a lesser—or smarter—man would have given up, I decided to give it one more try. Soccer season, here I come.

My enthusiasm almost lasted through the first practice. Actually, I knew I was in trouble even before the first practice, when I read the roster and noticed that my utterly skill-less basketball team made up nine of my 16 players. Things got worse at the parents' meeting. Theoretically, at this meeting you are supposed to get together with the parents of your players and discuss how they would be supportive and bring drinks and cheer and all that. In reality, this was where two of the parents told me they were happy to help, and the other fourteen threatened to beat me if their child did not score at least two goals a game. I did not think it was a prudent time to discuss the snack schedule.

As the practices progressed, I tried to teach my charges the basic skills of the game. Dribbling, passing, shooting, etc., the same skills I tried to teach my basketball team (and it didn't work then). It was truly amazing actually. The goal in soccer is something like one hundred twenty times larger than the goal in basketball, and these kids still couldn't get the ball anywhere *near* the damn thing.

Things got worse from there. Our first game began, and my young warriors, though they put up a valiant effort, trailed 17-0 at halftime. Every member of the team but one was called for a handball. The only member who didn't use his hands at all was the goalie. He did use the back of his head twice, but that didn't help much.

The following week I tried to correct as many of our shortcomings as I could. In seventeen hours of practice, I was able to get half the team to run without falling down, three quarters of the team to tie their own shoes, and three players to stop wearing their shin guards on their elbows. That was as far as we got, and the next game was apparently the first recorded triple-digit score in the history of our soccer league.

The week following that debacle I spent all of our practice time trying to instill the importance of playing your assigned position. This was because at one point in the previous game, I had noticed that of my eleven players, only the goalie and one halfback were even close to where they should have been. Two of my players were in the correct locations, *but on the wrong field* and I couldn't really count that. I drew diagrams. I walked them through it. I mailed detailed computer sketches to each and every one of their homes. I did everything I thought was humanly possible to explain to these developing young athletes the difference between a fullback and a forward, where a halfback lines up, and how far the center fullback could "roam." The later was important, because in our second game, our center fullback tried to "roam" to the McDonald's across the street. I thought that was too far, especially when the little monster didn't even bring me anything. I hoped and prayed that maybe, just maybe, I actually got through to them.

With our third game just minutes away, I called my ever-improving players around me. Only three of them had their shoes untied now. After a Vince Lombardi-type pep talk, during which one child asked if we were playing football, I called out the line up. This had been drafted at Hooter's the night before, over three pitchers of beer. That could explain why we almost put twelve players on the field, with two of them at quarterback, before we caught our mistake. Recovering, I told every one of them what position they were playing, then told them again. I even pointed it out on the easel I had stolen from the office, just to make sure. No sooner did I finish, and tell them to take the field, then seven little voices asked almost at once, "Coach, where am I?" Of the four who didn't ask, two of them lined up in the wrong spot anyway. I won't even go into the score of that one, but I didn't think it was possible to average a goal scored on us every forty seven seconds.

Every sports season brings new challenges, and this one was no different. In addition to losing every game by a deficit greater than the national debt (which

I was sadly becoming used to), my new challenge for this season was young female breasts.

Now, before you haul me off to the pedophile palace, let me explain. In soccer, there is something called a chest trap. This is where the player allows an airborne ball to hit him or her in the chest, so they can let it fall to the ground at their feet and control it. At least that's the way it is supposed to work. Most of my players hit the ball with their face, or else missed the ball entirely. Anyway, the practice after we showed our budding (which is *exactly* the word I want to use here) athletes how to chest trap, one of the parents pulled my female assistant coach aside and said that little Dolly wouldn't be doing chest traps anymore, as her breasts were developing, and it was just too painful.

My reaction as my assistant explained the situation to me later was one of sheer laughter, as this particular young athlete's form had ample padding: you could time her forty yard dash with a sundial. My assistant made me realize how insensitive I was being by kicking a ball at me in such a way that I had to demonstrate a "groin trap." I stopped laughing almost immediately. She, however, continued to laugh at me until the following Tuesday.

The season moved forward, our record spiraled downward, and in time, like a bad movie, it was finally over. At the end-of-season party, I tried to focus on the positive, like a good coach should. I almost succeeded, in that I actually opened my mouth and tried to speak. I still don't remember what actually came out. Something about "Well, at least no one got killed." Or something like that.

When it was all said and done, and the dust settled, the league commissioner asked me if I would be back next year. I laughed so hard I fell down.

I have decided to take some time off from coaching. Not long, just until this generation of kids is in high school, and can't hurt me anymore.

Honestly, Honesty Bites

This really happened. Afterwards, I swore I would never be this stupid again. I managed to keep that promise for about two years, and then did the same damn thing again. But that story appears later on. Keyword: Diane

❦   ❦   ❦

There are several things in life I have learned never to do. Sticking my tongue in an electrical outlet is near the top of that list, as is applying cologne to my privates. Both of these I learned at a young age. Recently, I added another important item to my ever increasing list of "do nots." Pay attention, guys, this one could save your life, and maybe, more importantly, your ego. Never, under any circumstances, even when threatened with a very painful death, openly express your deep personal feelings to a woman.

Usually, when offering advice of this nature, it is for one of two reasons. Either I have learned a very traumatic lesson, and want to prevent my readers from following in my bloody footsteps, or else I feel the unquenchable urge to tell the truth. In this case, it is neither. I am late for my publication deadline (again), but this may prove helpful anyway.

Recently, I flew down to Texas in order to see a certain young cowgirl. This girl was certainly one of a kind. She was gorgeous, intelligent, funny, gorgeous, rich, drove a cool car, smelled good, was really cute, and spoke to me. We had known each other when we were growing up, and because she had moved away, we had been writing back and forth. I needed a vacation, and it was either go see her or hang out with my grandparents. Since they are awake from noon to 1:38 PM each day, and their favorite pastime is denture cleaning, it was not a difficult choice. I figured while I was there, I might as well tell this goddess how I felt about her, and then we could get married and start a family before I had to be back to work.

In the movies when something like this happens, Warren Beatty pours his heart out to Madonna (oops, that's real life, let's start over). Tom Cruise pours out his heart to Kelly McGillis or some other such wonder-babe who up to this point has not spoken to him, or else has repeatedly slapped him, which I can totally relate to. If it's an R-rated movie, she gets all teary eyed and her heart gets moved and they go into a really great sex scene: if it is rated PG, the scene isn't all that great.

Now I learned at an early age that life is not like the movies (the whole "Superman" flying thing is still pretty painful), but even I didn't expect things to go as bad as they did.

I took her to dinner. I gazed into her eyes. I cleared the Big Mac wrappers from the table, held her hands, and let it all out. I told her everything. How she was the sun in my universe, the reason my world went 'round. How she was why I got up in the morning, and why I couldn't sleep at night. I mean, I threw every sappy quote from every Molly Ringwold movie ever made at this girl, trying to melt her heart. Well, her heart didn't exactly melt. It didn't even exactly budge. For a moment, I thought she was going to get up and walk out. I was only partially correct. She did get up, and then she ran *screaming* from the restaurant. Now *that* round trip ticket was money well spent.

My advice to my devout followers is: Find someone else to read. If I had any talent I would be doing something else. My advice to the rest of you, forget the honesty bit. Tell women exactly what they want to hear. You will score more, and probably get slapped less, at least until you get caught, at which point you are on your own.

I have had several chances to be honest with women since the Texas trip. I am happy to say I have taken exactly none of them. I lied, all the time, about everything. Even the little stuff. Brenda asked me if I liked pizza. I said no, even though I would sell my brother into slavery for a good slice of New York style. Jamie wanted to know if I enjoyed football. I said not really, even though I missed my first wedding because the Bears were on. Denise asked if I wanted to sleep with her. I said … well, OK, maybe I told the truth ONE time, but you should have seen Denise. It won't happen again though. Especially with Denise, as I lied about not seeing anyone else.

Video Game Reflections of the 1990's

One more reason why my "little" brother, who is 6'2" tall and outweighs me by 20 pounds, makes me nuts. I still love him though.

❦   ❦   ❦

Do you remember those Christmases growing up when there was just one toy that everyone *had* to have? One toy that was *so* cool that if you didn't get it you were damned to twelve months of living hell, anxiously awaiting the following Christmas in hopes of redemption? Growing up in the early eighties, that one toy one year was the Atari 2600 video game system.

For those of you not familiar with Atari 2600, I will explain. The Atari 2600 is to Sony Playstation® what either Cro-Magnon man or a New York Yankee fan is to modern man. The 2600 was actually a vast improvement over its predecessor, which was called Pong. Basically, Pong involved controlling a small white vertical line, hitting a small white square across a black screen, trying to get it past your opponent's vertical line. With the Atari 2600, you could actually insert different cartridges, each of which let you do different things with different sorts of lines. We used to stay up until all hours of the night playing different line games with our Atari 2600, and thinking how hi-tech it all was.

The other day I went home to visit my younger brother. He has a Playstation®, which is slightly more advanced than my old Atari. He wanted to play a fighting game, and I readily agreed. I remembered I had a fighting game for the good old Atari, where I could punch, kick, and even flip over potential aggressors. As our match began, I eagerly looked forward to educating my brother's character in the finer arts of pain. Well, for openers, my brother's character punched my character twice, kicked him in the throat three times, jumped over his head, spun around, *tore my character's arm off*, and proceeded to beat him with it. Immediately following that, my brother's warrior *froze* my warrior, and with a swift kick to the temple, *completely shattered his skull*. This took about seven seconds. I hadn't even gotten a good look at the screen yet, as I was still trying to figure out the eight buttons and four keys that are on the control pad. My trusty old Atari had a joystick with *one* button.

I immediately demanded a rematch, choosing the biggest, meanest character on the screen. This was another new experience, as in Atari you could be either Red, Blue, Black or White. Some games, you could just be just black or white. My brother picked a small lizard like creature, something along the lines of a cross between Richard Simmons and that stupid little amphibian from Frogger. Easy meat, I thought.

Well, for about the first six seconds, the fight was a draw. Frog boy slapped me once with his tongue, but I caught him with an uppercut when I accidentally dropped the control pad and it landed on one of the buttons. After that, I somewhat lost the initiative, as my brother stopped beating me with his tongue only long enough to kick me several times with his frog's apparently very powerful legs. For a finale, he grabbed me with his tongue, threw me up in the air, bicycle kicked me about eight times, sort of like a beach ball, and then kicked me through the ceiling. At this point, I was a little upset, and asked him how he beat me so easily. "Duh, you have to block," he said with a straight face.

I immediately demanded that we play another, less brutal game, like football. "OK," said my younger sibling, "do you want to play 'NFL Crush'Em,' 'NFL Black'n'Blue Division', or 'NFL Europe 2001?'" Whoa, all those choices? For the Atari we had the choice between "Football," where the field went top to bottom, and "Football," where the screen went left to right, and actually *scrolled* as you played—a major technological advance. I made a selection, and after twenty minutes and about forty-seven menus (quarter length, penalties, jock-strap color) we finally got to the coin toss. I lost; an omen for things to come.

My brother, to show what a great sport he was, kicked off. I promptly lost two yards on the return. On my next three plays, I fumbled, threw an incomplete pass to one of the cheerleaders, and got sacked for an 11-yard loss. On fourth down, I elected to punt, and promptly kicked the ball *behind* me. I recovered it in the end zone for a safety. On the kickoff, my brother ran it back for a touchdown, but not before injuring seven of my team's kickoff unit, three of them fatally. The final score was 98-0; 12 touchdowns, all with a two point conversion, plus the safety.

I won't even begin to go into what happened when we put in the driving game, but suffice to say that he will *never* drive with me again, and for my part, I am not ever going to loan him my car.

Not one to give up so easily, I went up into the attic, and after six hours of searching and falling through the ceiling only *one* time, I found my very own electronic fossil, the good old Atari 2600. We put in that age old favorite, "Combat", and selected "Jet Fighter vs. Jet Fighter" which looks like a red triangle and a blue triangle moving around the screen. Now he was on *my* turf, and I had him dead to rights.

He beat me 10-6.

Confessions Regarding Confessions

This story is special for a couple reasons. It is the only story I have ever written in one sitting, beginning to end. It is also the only story I ever wrote for a particular person. I was dating a wonderful woman named Cyndi, and at the time she had a fair amount of money, and I didn't. As the holidays approached, I began dropping hints that I would like to know what she might want for Christmas. My hints weren't all that subtle, and she finally just came out and said she wanted something "personal." "Why don't you write a story, just for me?" This story is the result, and I got the idea for it when I went to confession right before Christmas. Cyndi and I didn't work out (it was my fault, and for the record, I'm sorry I hurt her). But she's a wonderful person, and this story will always remind me of her.

❦　　　❦　　　❦

Let's start off by saying I'm Catholic. That's not a bad thing. I enjoy being Catholic. Catholicism may not be the perfect religion, but overall, it's not too bad. God has a sense of humor, and enjoys reminding me of that on an almost daily basis, and there's wine involved, so how bad could it be? Overall, I guess I give it an eight on a ten scale. It loses two points for being based primarily on guilt, but still, Islam doesn't let you eat pork, and Hindus worship cows, so I guess I'll keep it. Besides, if I convert, I have to start all over and get baptized again, and no way I am letting my parents dip me in cold water by my ankles in front of thirty relatives for a *second* time.

Anyway, one part of being Catholic is going to confession. Basically, confession is when you go to a priest, and tell him everything that you did wrong that you don't want to tell anyone except maybe the guys in the locker room. Then he counsels (yells) at you, makes you do a punishment called a "penance" and sends you on your merry way, free of sin until you flip off the first person who cuts you off in the parking lot.

Actually, that's not exactly the way it's supposed to work. The priest is supposed to provide guidance and wisdom in order to keep you from moving in with the devil. Unfortunately, lots of Catholics have had bad experiences during confessions, and because of that, confession has gotten a bad rap over the years.

Every Catholic has a bad confession story. Because I am an overachiever, I have three. My first bad confession story coincides exactly with my first confession. Because I went to a Catholic school, we diligently prepared for our first confessions from the first through the third grades. I also prepared a lot on my own, by committing numerous sins and then writing them down so when it was time to tell the priest I wouldn't leave anything out. The big day came, and I took a deep breath and entered "the confessional." There sat Father Riener, who was technically old enough to have been one of the original apostles. As I began reciting my list, Father began falling asleep. Being only in the fourth grade, I did exactly what I did at home when my younger sister fell asleep. I kicked him.

Father immediately awoke and began haranguing me on how I was going straight to hell without even passing go or receiving $200 for raising my hand to a religious person. At this point I didn't think it necessary to correct him, even though it was actually my foot. I was shaken, and for years distrusted all priests and nuns, and also penguins due to the resemblance. On the bright side, for making my first confession, several of my relatives gave me money, which is the way Italian families celebrate everything, including breakfast.

My second bad confession involved me arguing with a priest. The particular sin in question occurred when I "accidentally" found one of my Dad's *Playboy* magazines by "accidentally" looking for it. My Dad happens to collect *Playboy*, and has every issue ever published, which made me very popular with my friends when I was growing up. I found one, and looked through it a few (seventeen) times. Being a good Catholic I of course felt guilty afterwards, and confessed all this at my next confession the following Tuesday. In the Catholic school I went to, they gave us the opportunity to go to confession every other week. If we didn't, we failed religion class. The priest explained to me why looking at beautiful naked women was wrong, and then told me to throw all the offensive material away. I personally did not find beautiful naked women particularly offensive, but this was not the time to bring that up. The bigger problem was that my Dad had literally *hundreds* of *Playboy*s worth *thousands* of dollars, so I explained that throwing them all away might be tricky to do without some help, and possibly a U-haul. The priest then decided that I only needed to throw *some* of the magazines away. I then decided that such action would probably get me killed, in which case my Dad would have to go to confession, and the priest might tell my Dad all the stuff I told the priest, and then I would *really* be in trouble. I refused. The torments of the afterlife did not scare me anywhere near as much as my father did. The priest rolled his eyes, gave me a penance of something like forty-seven Our Fathers, to be said while standing naked in the snow at my bus stop, and sent me on my way.

My third bad confession story was just last year. I went to my parish penance service, and after we sang songs and thought really hard about all the things we really didn't want to tell the priest, it was time for the main event. The parish pastor introduced the priests he brought in to assist him with hearing confessions. They were Father O'Malley, Father O'Leary, Father O'Sullivan, and Father MacNamara. I, as you know, am very much Italian. "Father, forgive me for I have sinned. I didn't root for Notre Dame to win the national championship …"

With these stories on my conscience, you can understand why I was a little hesitant to go to the penance service this year. Still, I sucked up the courage, and went. As I stood there outside and waited to go into the confessional, I went over everything that I was going to tell the priest in my mind, reminding myself to make sure I looked appropriately repentant, since pity points count. I alphabetize my sins, and had only gotten through the L's, when it was my turn.

I went in. I took a deep breath. I laid it all out. Everything I had done wrong since my last confession. Father didn't bat an eye. When I was done, I braced myself for Father's onslaught. And I got …

Nothing. Father blessed me, gave me my penance (say two prayers and wink at the nun on way out), and sent me on my way. This had to have been the most stress free confession ever.

Instead of being relieved, I was actually pretty upset. If I had known it was going to be that easy, I would have listed stuff that I planned to do in the future, just to get credit for it later. I really felt cheated, and began to get irate. "Listen, Bucko, you better start telling me how to live my life, and don't skimp on the celibacy stuff, either." He just looked at me, crossed himself, and asked Brother Bruno to "counsel" me. Brother Bruno played defensive end at Georgetown. I quickly saw the light (and stars).

I haven't had anything to feel guilty about lately, and I feel kind of guilty about that, so maybe I need to go to confession again. Of course, if Brother Bruno is still around, maybe conversion isn't such a bad idea.

Reincarnation Ramblings

The second story inspired by Cindy. I actually don't know if I believe in this stuff, but it does make you think.

❦　　　❦　　　❦

Once upon a time, a now ex-girlfriend of mine introduced me to the concept of reincarnation. We were just sitting there, watching TV, when she suddenly asked if I thought we had met before. Because I was watching Monday Night Football at the time, I merely nodded my head and grunted my agreement, having as usual no real concept of what she was saying or why she was even trying to speak to me on a Monday night during the regular season. She took my agreement as permission to launch into a discussion of the great mystery of past lives. I was also pondering a great mystery, namely why the Bears would call a quarterback sneak on fourth and seventeen, but this was obviously very important to her. Because it was almost halftime, and because I didn't want to sleep on the couch, I began to listen.

She began to tell me about this great book that she read which described three people: a man and a woman, and their therapist. To briefly summarize a story that apparently was written through the course of time (or, more likely, the haze of alcohol), the man and the woman had been in love with each other several times spanning many hundreds of years, and were always tragically separated. Sometimes one was a man and one a woman, or a mother and a son, or maybe a father and daughter, or possibly the President and a White House intern. But the important theme tying all the stories together was that there was always some kind of tragic separation.

These two people, who did not know each other "in this life," were profoundly unhappy, and began to see this therapist for treatment, and also because throwing their money in a hole in a ground seemed too easy a method of disposal. As this doctor examined his notes, he began to realize that he could really ride these folks for a lot of money, and so treated each of them for unhappiness through many years.

Part of the treatment was regression therapy. In regression therapy, the doctor hypnotizes you and you admit to being someone else in another life, but you don't remember it when you are awake and trying to deal with the hassles of this life. Anyway, as the story goes, the doctor realized, as he continuously regressed these two people, that they were telling two sides of the same story, and that they must meet so they could fall madly in love, and then he could charge them for couple's therapy too. They met, fell madly in love, and lived happily ever after.

To be honest, I am having trouble believing this. I have trouble remembering people I went out with *last week*, and I am supposed to believe that these folks remember each other from centuries ago? I expressed my feelings to my companion, and promptly got the "You are sleeping on the couch," face. *That* I remember, having seen it so often.

I don't know if you have noticed, folks, but the world is a pretty big place. Am I supposed to believe that several times throughout history I may have met the same person over and over and over again? In a world this big? And how do I know that that person hasn't spent all those generations trying to *avoid* me? There is just too much to swallow with the whole concept.

"But what about all the *evidence*?" my companion asked. "What about the man who was killed by a lion, and then in his next life didn't like cats?" I got news for you, doll face. I don't believe in this reincarnation stuff, and I still hate cats.

If I understand this correctly, in addition to dating, keeping the house clean, jock itch, and a host of other things the modern male needs to worry about, now I have the added concern of worrying that whatever I do right or wrong in this life may not just affect the here and now, but also the there and later. No, no pressure there. "Gee, I hope I don't screw this dinner date up, in case it ruins *her next three lifetimes*."

Like so many other of my relationships, this one ended. She said she couldn't be with anyone who did not share her beliefs about starting over, but that in a future life, she would be willing to date me again if I became "enlightened" and saw the error of my ways. I politely commented that she need not worry about it, as the one error I didn't plan on repeating in this life or any other was speaking to her ever again.

I have decided not to worry about being reincarnated. I have actually started planning for it, just in case. I have started several bank accounts, each with initially very puny sums of money. The account numbers I have written on a slip of paper, which I plan to pass down to my ancestors, without telling them what they are. That way, when I come back in 200 years or so, I simply need to look them up and cash in on the interest. It's a long shot, but the return on investment could be *huge*.

Life With My Parents

This one has always gotten mixed reviews, but it's still one of my favorites. Unlike some of my others, it's as true now as the day I wrote it. I hope my kids feel this way about me when I'm a parent.

❊   ❊   ❊

It's funny how my relationship with my parents went through stages.

First there was the totally dependent stage. My parents fed me, clothed me, changed my diapers, burped me, bathed me, and protected me from monsters that lived in my closet. My area of responsibility was crying, spitting up, making cute little cooing sounds and occasionally banging some pots and pans together. Both parties carried out their duties with exceptional zeal.

Next came the not-so-totally-but-pretty-close-to-it dependent stage, when I was in elementary school. My parents still fed me, clothed me, and protected me from monsters that lived in the closet. They also started giving me advice and teaching me. For my part, I still was in charge of crying, but took on the additional responsibilities of taking out the garbage and washing the car. Occasionally, I still banged pots and pans together too.

Junior High brought the still-pretty-dependent-but-starting-to-pull-away stage. My parents still fed me and clothed me and taught me, but girls replaced monsters in causing my sleepless nights. I still cried (less, but it still happened), took out the garbage, and washed the car. I also babysat my brother and sister, cut the grass, took care of the pool, and only rarely banged pots and pans together.

High school filled me with wisdom. As a result, I entered the feel-like-I-am-totally-independent-but-really-I-am-not stage, where I felt like I was ready to be my own self-sufficient person. In truth, my parents still fed me and clothed me and drove me on dates until I got my license. I still mowed the grass and took out the garbage and generally felt like I was indispensable around the house and therefore *must* be ready to be on my own. I was obviously *not* going to bang pots and pans together, now that I was so close to being out of the house.

College brought the total independence stage. Lots of college students can't say that (Mom and Dad still pay the tuition, so that sounds pretty dependent), but I went to a federal service academy where tuition was free. I only relied on my parents for moral support, as the government provided for all my material needs (at least it provided everything it decided I needed). Finally, I was totally independent from my parents. I didn't have time to bang pots and pans together.

Graduation arrived after four arduous years that lasted a forever that went into extra innings. My first act of any importance as a commissioned officer of the United States Navy was to rear-end the nicest old lady in New Providence, New Jersey only days after canceling the collision insurance on my car. It was my first auto accident ever. Up until then, I had never even gotten a speeding ticket. You know what I did?

I called my parents. I even almost cried. I really loved that car. It felt like I just maimed my best friend.

Independence does not mean isolation. I was getting the two confused in my head for a while. I am glad I got it straight.

Where am I now? Well, I feed myself, clothe myself (according to Navy regulations, of course), burp myself, bathe myself, and deal with monsters and girls by myself. I also take out the trash and wash the car. Someone else mows the grass and I have my own pots and pans. I call home at least twice a week. I guess you could call it the I-am-out-on-my-own-but-I-hope-you-will-always-be-there-for-me stage.

Both parties still carry out their duties with exceptional zeal.

Love and the Video Store

No matter how "in love" a couple is, renting a movie can be a major test of a rela-
tionship. "Well of course I want to be with you, honey, I just don't want to be with
you and have to suffer through a movie about a waitress who finds love by going to
church with her mom."

❧   ❧   ❧

There are several things in our everyday lives that can test the modern relationship. Whether or not she puts the cap on the toothpaste, or if he leaves the
toilet seat up. How many times she needs to be cuddled. How often he brings
other women home.

However, none of these come close to that ultimate test of a couple's true
love; renting a movie. I know, it sounds harmless. A guy and a girl who are
obviously madly in love (known each other six days, sleeping together for five,
and he almost knows her last name) walk into a movie store. Immediately, they
together begin searching for a title, separately.

It's like a chess game. Moving a pawn, the guy tests her defenses with *Bottom of the Ninth*, a sports classic about a minor leaguer struggling to make it to
the big leagues by hitting a home run with the female team owner. The woman
counters his attack with a move by her knight entitled *Cuddle Me Forever*, a
sappy flick seemingly devoted to every part of a relationship except sex (which,
ironically, is the only part the guy really wants to watch). Our hero probes
again, more boldly this time, perhaps a move with a bishop, or his own knight,
with *Bare-Chested Bikini Babes Unchained*, a cheeky work about one southern
college's sorority activities. She quashes this thrust with *Tenderness*, an unbe-
lievably long movie which seems to involve a man, a woman, a picnic basket, a
riverbank, and no plot beyond this poor idiot pouring his guts out to a woman

the viewers are convinced doesn't know he exists (sadly, I can relate). Stud man panics, and tries feebly to counter with a sport documentary. She laughs as she deploys her pieces, King Lear, Queen Cleopatra, Sir Lancelot, and a host of Oscar winners. Finally, she offers him *Feelings*, a mushy story in which the woman gets the man to submit to her every whim by using the bold tactic of asking nicely. At this point the woman also reminds the most recent love of her life that post-movie physical activity, and not the kind in *Rambo, Part VII*, usually involves two people, and watching *Earnest Visits a Nudist Colony* might not put her in the mood. Checkmate.

As painful as the above scenario sounds, I would still prefer it over what happened to me the last time I tried to rent a movie with that special someone (defined as "she who was speaking to me that week"). We walked into the store, and within five minutes I knew I was in trouble. Apparently, this young lady had spent every night for the past six years in a movie theater, because she had seen absolutely *everything* I suggested. Dramas, westerns, war films, foreign films (*Ernest visits a DUTCH Nudist Colony*), she had seen them all. Finally, in a moment of sheer desperation, I blurted, "Well, is there anything you *haven't* seen?" Big mistake, as we ended up watching *All Time Greatest Foreign Infomercials, Volume II*; she had already seen the first one.

Personally, I think movie stores are set up all wrong anyway. You walk in, and there are about seventeen different categories you are expected to look through before you make a selection, and any movie you are looking for can be filed under up to four different categories anyway. When you finally find one that even remotely interests you, it has already been rented. This happens most often in the "New Releases" section, which averages six actual movies per 150 movie boxes on the shelves at any given time. Except Friday night, when the number is closer to three.

My latest squeeze wanted to rent a movie the other day. Not wanting to play a game I always lose, I backed out, and suggested we do something more "stimulating". She suggested chess, and then beat me in seven moves. Hooray for the modern relationship.

The Very First Family Fun Night

I sort of miss Family Fun Night now, but they got off to sort of an inglorious beginning...

✦   ✦   ✦

I'll have to tell this story second-hand, because even though I was there, I was only about three-and-a-half years old, so my memory is a little foggy.

Back in 1975, my parents, fresh off their first new car (a 1974 Cadillac) and their second new child (my sister) decided that it was time for a family night out. We voted on it, but because I wasn't yet four and my sister not yet one year, our votes really didn't count that much, especially since I voted for a banana and my sister voted to drool. My parents won easily, and it was time to go.

We piled into the new car, which I can honestly say without exaggeration was bigger than both my first apartment and the state of Rhode Island. Therefore, we had plenty of room. For this glorious "Ballister Family Fun Night" my parents had elected to go to that icon of yesteryear entertainment, the drive-in movie.

For the younger readers, you might not recognize what a drive-in is, as most of them went out of business around the same time that VCR's became popular. It was at that time that people figured out that if they were going to be hot, tired, uncomfortable, and have a limited view of the screen, they might as well do it in the comfort of their own home. Also, cars were a lot bigger back then, and so there was much more room to party like naked monkeys in the back seat than in today's vehicles. I have never even *been* in the back seat of my late-model truck, as I don't fit and couldn't possibly expect anyone else to.

In order to make the event pleasing to both the parents and the children, my parents elected to go to the movie "Bambi." They would be happy because they could drive their new car to the movie and sit in it all night, and we would be happy because it was a cartoon featuring a skunk and a deer. Off we went to enjoy the evening.

While they did put a lot of thought into the evening, my dear parents neglected to take into account some important factors, such as the weather, my sister's inability to sit still, and the sensitivity of a three-year-old child.

Things didn't start to go wrong until after the opening credits ended. That's about when we noticed that when you turn the car off, the air conditioning goes off as well. This was New Jersey in July, so the temperature and humidity were about 99 degrees and 98 percent, respectively. As we started to sweat off dinner, my nine-month old sister, for no other reason than she happened to be nine months old, started to cry. Loudly, and with no intention of stopping, despite numerous attempts and copious amounts of baby-talk from my parents. God blessed my sister with an incredible set of lungs, so not only could we not hear the movie, but neither could people anywhere in the vicinity of our vehicle. I simply tried ignoring her (I kept trying throughout junior high) and rolled my eyes the way all worldly three-and-a-half-year-olds do.

Finally, she stopped crying, and, deciding she was bored, began crawling all over the car. Now, because the vehicle was large enough inside to actually have its own weather patterns, she was able to cover a lot of ground. She was in the front seat, she was in the back seat, she was messing with the speaker, she was in the trunk, she was draining the oil; in short, she was *everywhere*. My parents made attempts to corral her, but each time she would give them her withering "if you dare stop me I'll cry some more" face, and that settled that. We went back to melting and let her enjoy her run of the sauna vehicle from Hell.

And then tragedy struck. Bambi's mother died. Despite being a worldly three-and-a-half-year-old, the sadness of the moment overcame me, and I began to cry. It didn't help that my sister was biting me at the moment, but that was of secondary concern. At this point, my parents had enough, and decided that this family fun night out with the kids would best be concluded at home with the children in bed. Dad peeled rubber, and we exited the parking lot throwing gravel. In his zeal, we forgot to take the speaker out of the car. We tried to take it back to the drive-in some time later, but like all drive-ins, it was closed. We still have it.

My family never returned to the drive-in. Actually, it was several years before we embarked on family fun nights of any kind. It was several more years before they abandoned their moratorium on having more children and my brother came along. His behavior as a baby resulted in Family Fun Nights being eliminated all together, but that's a story for another time.

The Return of Mr. Chang

The scariest part of this story is that every bit of this one is true!

🍁   🍁   🍁

You may remember the story of my very first business trip, and all the trials and tribulations of dealing with Mr. Chang. If you don't, picture taking a business trip to Hell accompanied by your mother in-law, a screaming infant, and the chairman of the Democratic convention. Multiply that by about seventeen, and then shove bamboo shoots under your fingernails and light them on fire. That's pretty much what it was like traveling with Mr. Chang.

That trip was shortly after Mr. Chang began working in our office. Since that time, he has continued to make virtually everyone either miserable or crazy (except for the boss, who was already both). His exploits have become legendary, and have spread across our company faster then the fire he accidentally set three weeks ago. I can still hear him saying, "Oh, yu not supposed to cwean off da hot coffee pot wit gazowine? I not know dat." Some of his misadventures have been harmless, meaning no loss of life and property loss not in excess of $250. Others have been both more spectacular and more financially distasteful to the office.

In his job, Mr. Chang occasionally must visit remote areas. This is not unusual for our office, and we have several four-wheel-drive vehicles available for such events. Recently, as he was leaving the office with the keys to our newest trail handling vehicle in his hand, he said that he would use his "goot chudgment" to determine how remote an area he would visit that day. Of course, when he said this, it took the better part of an hour. I said nothing, just glad to have him out of the office for a while, because I never get much done when he is around. Mr. Chang came to my desk one Tuesday morning and started a conversation that ended sometime the following Thursday afternoon.

Anyway, around lunch time I noticed that I had not been interrupted at all that morning, and began to wonder (happily) if maybe His Flatulence had just kept going, and wasn't coming back. Sadly, it was not to be as he came limping through the door soon after, completely bedraggled but nevertheless alive. Seeing that he was alive, and not having the two hours and 16 minutes necessary to hear his story, I quickly left for a meeting, taking for granted that if he was back and reasonably in one piece, than the vehicle probably was too.

About three hours later, my supervisor asked me where the brand new truck was. I answered that it must be in the lot, as Mr. Chang had been back for hours. My boss politely informed me that the truck was most certainly *not* in the parking lot, and that if I didn't find it before I went home, there would really be no need for me to come back, ever. I immediately sought out Mr. Chang to find out where he had put the truck, and also to see what other valuable property he had managed to destroy that day.

Even the short version of the story, as told by Mr. Chang, would take volumes, so I will summarize. Apparently, Mr. Chang drove the vehicle down a path that was not wide enough to be navigated by mountain goats, and got it stuck. As he got out of the vehicle to ponder his predicament ("O, I guess itz stuwck."), he was immediately attacked by bees, who were apparently upset at having their home stomped upon by a ranting immigrant with zero command of the English language. Apparently, these were very patriotic bees. Mr. Chang fled the scene, and by the time he recovered his composure, he had traveled a fair distance and was unable to locate the vehicle. As he began walking out of the woods, he came upon a good natured fellow named Moe walking in the other direction. After an insightful conversation of about forty-one seconds, Mr. Chang gave the keys to our brand new vehicle to this Good Samaritan and continued on his way, finally stopping at the local stables, where he called the office for a ride. Upon arriving back at the office, he neglected to tell anyone in the office that the vehicle was still missing in action. "O, shud I have mentioned dat?"

While my initial instinct was to throttle this individual, in a brief moment of clarity I realized that if I were to kill him, no matter how satisfying that would be, I would probably never find the missing vehicle. As a result I would be fired, and as a result would be dumped by my girlfriend, who continued to go out with me only because I paid her to do so. Mr. Chang and I immediately departed for the woods.

Fifteen minutes after we left, I seriously regretted my decision not to kill King Fossil. As we meandered our way through trails I would be scared to drive a main battle tank through, Mr. Chang alternated between knowing exactly where we were and not having an idea what state we were in. At one point *everything* would look familiar: "Oh, yeah, I definutwy wuz here." One hundred yards later, he would just shake his head sadly and mutter, "Oh, I not dink I wuz here."

There was a glimmer of hope when we came to a junction of five trails out in the middle of what can only be described as "nowhere." Mr. Chang lit up like a roman candle, spewing flaming hot bastardized English in all directions. Loosely translated, he recognized the place. "I wuz here, I wuz here, I know dat I wuz here!" he joyfully exclaimed. OK, I thought, finally some progress.

"Mr. Chang," I began, whispering a silent prayer that *all* his brain cells weren't crystallized with old age, "now just tell me which direction you went."

He pondered. He thought hard. He thought *really* hard. He popped two of his remaining blood vessels, but finally he answered. "Oh, I not wemembew. Maybe weft. Maybe not. It so confwusing." At this point I just about lost it, as evidenced by the fact that my face turned beet red and I could not speak anything close to comprehensible speech. As smoke poured from my ears, I drove back to our building, only once seriously considering parking on the railroad tracks. I was just about beyond caring about my boss, my job, or the possibility of twenty-five to life for homicide.

Later that evening, after I had a chance to cool down, a buddy and I went back into the woods to look for our missing vehicle. After about four hours of searching, we found it about 25 yards from an area where Mr. Chang stated, "Oh, it not anywhere near here. I wuz nowhere near dis spot." Despite the proclamation of His Eminence that, "It weally stuck. It not coming out. Not in hundwed yeaws," we were able to free the vehicle with the ingenious plan of actually putting the vehicle in four-wheel drive and hitting the gas pedal. It popped out like a greased hog on ice.

Mr. Chang pretty much made local history that day. All the office was talking about it, and if they didn't hear about it that day, that piece on the five o'clock news that evening was pretty popular. And the local paper the next morning.

But his exploits don't stop there. Mr. Chang always has a scheme; some way that he is going to get rich in a hurry with minimal effort "awftu he wetiwes." (After he retires? Geez, the man is seventy eight and a half *now*.) First, he was going to teach Chinese to American businessmen. Then, he was going to buy and sell real estate. Now, after hearing about my vacation cruise with my family, his latest scheme is to work on a cruise ship as a bartender "cowecting tips from stupid owd bizness women who just want my body."

When he was not scheming, or losing company vehicles, or attempting to set the world record for consecutive sneezes, he was supposed to be working. This involved using his computer, with which, according to his application, he was infinitely familiar. Having met him, I doubt he can spell either infinitely *or* familiar, and what's more, he didn't know how to use a computer anymore than he knew how to use the English language.

This was never more clear as the time he called me into his office to help him with a computer problem. He was having difficulty installing something from a CD ROM. It took me only a few seconds to find the root of the problem. Captain Ancient had shoved the CD into the 5 ¼" drive. ("Oh, I tot it went in kind o tight.") At this point I was seriously regretting my personal decision not to bring firearms to work.

We have several customers that we deal with in the course of our business day. The ones we care about, I meet with. The ones we are trying to get back at, or we have a grudge with, we allow Mr. Chang to meet with. Usually, they are no longer our customers after that. We almost always get a written note commenting on Mr. Chang's performance. One of the more recent ones said: "Your employee was twenty minutes late to our meeting. After he arrived, we got considerably less done than we had while he was absent. There was also violence requiring armed police response. Please do not send him to anymore meetings." Another note used slightly less professional language. It was also attached to a brick.

The other day Mr. Chang announced his plans to quit. In his own words "I'm tu goot fo dis pwace. I need tu find anudder job wher dey appweciate my tawents." Though I can't think of anyone that would appreciate his talents of punctual gas passing and driving everyone he makes contact with insane, I nevertheless wished him luck.

Two days later, he told us he found another job. Same location. Better pay. A promotion really. Mr. Chang is now my boss.

I Knew Just Enough Spanish to be Dangerous

As a naval officer, I've gotten to do lots of traveling. Sometimes, it's to places most people wouldn't want to go, but all in all it has been an educational and wonderful experience. What follows is the first of two writings inspired when my unit deployed to Spain.

❦   ❦   ❦

For the first time in my not so young life, I got to spend an extended period of time in a foreign country when my military unit was deployed overseas. There are obviously several exciting things about a foreign land. New people, new women, foreign food, different culture, and the list goes on and on. Of course, it is a lot easier to enjoy these things when you can understand the language. As I have a hard enough time with English, you can imagine the difficulties I was facing.

To my rescue rode my buddy Miguel. Miguel's parents happened to come from Spain, which happened to be the foreign land we were visiting, and he grew up speaking Spanish. Under normal conditions, you would think that this would be a good thing, but Miguel had a "different" sense of humor, and thought it was funny to get the rest of us in trouble. On numerous occasions at work, one or the other of us has been left on the receiving end of one of his little jokes. But, as he was the only one in my unit who spoke the native language fluently, we had no choice but to trust him.

The first time we went out among the local Spanish culture, we ended up in a restaurant. It was a *very* Spanish restaurant, meaning the staff did not speak even one word of English. The only way we were going to eat was if we ordered in Spanish. No problem, Miguel was with us. We told him what we wanted, and he rattled off some words in Spanish so fast I thought he sprained his tongue. The waitress rattled some things off with equal speed, and off she went.

Miguel's meal arrived, and was a succulent Spanish delicacy with all the trimmings, served by a gorgeous dancing Spanish girl. I and one other member of our party, John, began smacking our lips, as we had asked Miguel to order us the exact same thing. The last member of our group, Steve, was equally impressed, and also looked forward to the meal.

Well, the rest of our food arrived, and we soon realized that Miguel was really enjoying himself, at our expense. My dinner and John's did not look anything alike, and certainly did not look like Miguel's meal. Nor were they served by a beautiful Spanish dancing girl. John's was actually served by a man wearing what looked like a chemical protection suit. I am not really sure what Steve's dinner looked like, but I do know that it appeared to be looking back at him. Miguel fell on the floor laughing, and then ran out and left us with the bill.

We (meaning Miguel) all had a good laugh over that one. He wasn't laughing so hard when I tied him up and put him in the closet, though. My thirst for revenge slated, I proceeded out in to town, *sans* Miguel, for another fun-filled evening. The fact that none of the group I brought with me spoke anything more than a smattering of Spanish was pretty much forgotten.

We arrived at a bar and immediately set about mingling with the locals. There were five of us—*cinco* in Spanish. First there was James, a large "good ol' boy" from the great state of Texas. He was six foot three inches tall, and weighed about as much as a Volkswagen. As such, he was two and a half times the size of the average Spanish man. Next was Larry. He was slightly taller than James, but weighed a lot less. In addition, he was black, and was wearing an LA Lakers shirt (that will become important later). Next up was John, a veteran of the above-described restaurant affair, who happened to be a doctor. Finally, there was Steve and myself, who had no special skills or qualities whatsoever.

We began drawing attention to ourselves almost immediately. First of all, we had arrived in a military vehicle, a solid piece of American machinery known as a Blazer, painted a most attractive shade of olive drab green. Its big diesel engine had not been tuned up since the First Gulf War, and it could be heard throughout most of Southwestern Europe. It was also twice the size of any vehicle ever made in Spain, and about six inches wider than several of the streets in the town. It was not possible to park this beast without being on the curb or sidewalk on at least one side of the street.

Added to our subtle entrance was the fact that James and Larry were perhaps the two tallest individuals in the entire town. The women had never seen such large individuals, and Larry's size and attire gave him instant celebrity status as an American basketball legend—a misperception we did not try to correct. Women were gathering all around to stare in awe at him, and for absolutely no reason were jumping into his arms. So far, we were doing pretty well for some *Americanos estupidos*.

Our stock rose even higher when John busted out with "Yo estoy el doctor (I am a doctor)," one of the few phrases he knew and could pronounce correctly. The other was "This chicken is excellent," and didn't really seem appropriate given the situation. Now began the difficulties, as we were forced to actually attempt verbal communication.

Of all the members in the group, only myself and John had ever had any Spanish classes. Steve and Larry had taken French in high school, and James spoke only Texan. I had been working with Steve, trying to teach him to say the phrase "Hola, mi nombre es Steve," which translates as "Hello, my name is Steve." He did well in practice, but dropped the ball at game time. The literal translation of what he said, "Hola, mi *hombre* es Steve," was "Hello, my man is Steve," which instantly gave all the lovely Spanish girls the impression that Steve, and the rest of us by association, were gay. We decided to move to a different bar and start over.

At our next stop, we sat down for some refreshment. I stepped up to try and order from memory some Spanish appetizers. The literal translation of what I ordered was toast with cheese and soap, and fish testicles on a rock. After the waiter got off the floor (Spanish people can laugh really hard) he brought us an English menu, and we humbly ordered.

Things steadily got worse from there, as our inadequate language skills got us into more and more trouble. The low point was when Steve, trying to express his true feelings towards a woman he just met, told her she was *muy guapo*, which means "very handsome." Being called a man was a bit much for this young lady to deal with, and, as families in Spain are very close, she immediately told her father and two very large brothers, who came looking for us in order to "educate" us on Spanish customs. We quickly vamoosed from the scene, and when we arrived home, we immediately sought out Miguel from the closet and came to terms with him for any future excursions. Basically, he owns us, and in return, he won't sell us into slavery.

Though we wouldn't sample the nightlife any more without Miguel to act as an interpreter, Steve and I did try to take on the local shopping mall by ourselves. We had been "in-country" three weeks by this point, and felt our Spanish had improved at least enough to keep us from getting arrested. We moved about the mall rather easily, and it really wasn't much different from an American mall except for the fact that no one spoke English. Steve was still a little hesitant to use any Spanish, especially after the beautiful-woman-handsome-man incident described earlier, so the talking was left up to me.

We were having quite an enjoyable afternoon when we walked into this little gift shop, where two very lovely young Spanish ladies were working. I was actually able to get the point across that we were two Americans, and that we didn't speak much Spanish. Apparently I also told her that we were both huge suckers, because she immediately tried to sell us anything I even glanced at. Normally, I would have just walked out, but this girl was both incredibly good looking and talking to me (albeit in a language I did not understand) and I was in no hurry to end the encounter. The bottom line was I ended up spending the equivalent of twelve American dollars on a ceramic mole. Yes, a mole, or *tupa* in Spanish. This was no ordinary mole, though. This mole was flat on his back, wearing boxing gloves and trunks (of course). I had no idea what this pugilistic mole represented, nor what I was going to do with it. Further proof that men will do incredibly stupid things for two breasts and a pretty smile.

One part of Spanish culture we wanted to sample as soon as possible (before we got ourselves deported) was a bullfight. In addition to the fact that it was something unique to Spain, as an added bonus there would be lots of Spanish women to flirt with. We piled into the van at the first opportunity.

Spain is an old country. Pretty much every building in Spain, even the "new" ones, are pretty old. The bullfighting arena, or "Plaza de Torros" (literally, "Place Where Young Men Try Very Hard Not to Get Poked in the Butt by a Bull") was no exception. The old New York City Polo Grounds, which have long since been torn down and bulldozed and turned into something not even remotely resembling a ballpark, is *still* a more modern sports facility than the bullfighting arena we went to. These facilities were way beyond primitive. There were NO snack bars, we sat on concrete bleachers, there was no PA system, and the bathrooms looked like outhouses except that they were inside. However, there were lights, presumably for those twilight doubleheader bullfights.

Before the bullfights even began, there was a parade. This involved everyone who would participate in the bullfight, except the bulls. Following that, the first fight began. For those of you who picture bullfighting as the ultimate confrontation between man and beast, where the brave matador faces down the heaving, pawing bull, stop reading. The truth might break your hearts. What really happens is that while the matador is still pulling on his really tight pants (how does he *move* in those things?), the bull is being worked over by something like seven other junior varsity matadors. After that, two armored horses with mounted *picadores* (literally, "those who ride the armored horses") run and poke and prod the bull almost to exhaustion. Then the matador comes in for the final kill and all the glory. In Spain, it is actually impolite to cheer for the bull. This is one reason everyone is so happy at bullfights. They must cheer for the matador, and he never loses.

This nine-on-one action offends my American sense of fair play, and also robs me of my right to root for the underdog. I think that something along the lines of six on six would be much more fair to the bulls, and at the same time much more amusing for everyone to watch.

I mentioned this to someone, and he spouted off a long blast of Spanish that went over both my head and my rudimentary Spanish by about 30 feet. Miguel later told me that what he said, loosely translated, was "Wait until Easter." So I did.

What happens at Easter in Spain is commonly referred to as the "Running of the Bulls." This great Spanish tradition allows those individuals who desire to be chased by an enraged bull, but lack the discipline and training to become matadors, to realize their dreams and possibly end up in the emergency room. The gist of event is that the local town governments release live, wild, exceedingly pissed off bulls into the streets and let them chase various Spanish people all around town. People come from miles around for the privilege of being chased and possibly gored by the bulls. Further, to prove their bravery and make it even easier for the bulls, the people usually drink themselves into oblivion *before* allowing themselves to be chased by the bulls.

As witness to this, I remember being amazed that all the participants weren't killed. My second thought was that if they were stupid enough to drink themselves silly and then get in the street with a huge, snorting, upset bull, they really didn't deserve to live anyway. Be that as it may, it was certainly fun to watch; especially because anyone who survives resumes drinking themselves silly in a block party that makes Mardi Gras look like evening tea.

Eventually, deployment ended, and we were rotated back to the states, robbing the Spanish government of the chance to deport us. Many of us learned some useful Spanish. Some of us made lifelong friends. Two of us learned what words Spanish policeman use for "Why are you urinating in the street, you stupid American?"

Spain is very different from the United States. But when you bear in mind that they have excellent bread, great wine, and all the women are gorgeous and only allowed to wear skin tight pants, the differences become less important.

I'd go back; whether or not they would have me is a different story. Next time, I'm rooting for the bull.

Halloween in Spain

Here's the second foreign country story. I will never go through a Halloween again without remembering this party ...

❦   ❦   ❦

Halloween has always been a good time for me. Anytime that ugliness is espoused and even celebrated, I usually fit right in. So when a friend of mine invited us to a Halloween party while we were deployed to Spain, we all jumped at the chance to go.

Being on deployment in a foreign country, our costume choices were somewhat limited. We didn't have enough of anything to make a theme for the six of us, so we had to improvise. The only thing we did have in abundance was sheets, so in typical cool guy fashion, we did the toga thing, and capped it off with real leaf wreaths. We looked incredibly studly (or really stupid, but it was Halloween, and either would suffice).

We piled into the van, all of us dressed in our sheets except Leaping Larry, who was running late as usual and said he would just apply his sheets when we parked the van before we went inside. We packed up our contribution to the party—two cases of beer—and off we went. One thing our host failed to mention, which we discovered only when we reached the general vicinity of the party, was that there was absolutely no parking anywhere *near* the party. Therefore, we had to walk about three blocks to the party from where we parked. Before we could even do that, Larry had to change.

Now, earlier, when we parked the van on this narrow Spanish back street, there was absolutely no one to be seen. Ten minutes later, with the six foot six inch Larry outside wrapping himself in bed sheets, and five other guys wearing similar sheets with wreaths on their heads in the van right behind him, it was like a New York City rush hour. There were hundreds of people roaring by in their little ugly European cars or else rocketing by on their mopeds. Though hurtling along at incredible speeds, none of them failed to give some sort of reaction to *los Americanos locos.* We saw several facial expressions, ranging from amazement to utter disbelief. We also saw several unique international finger gestures, but we won't talk about those.

Finally, Larry was ready, and we dismounted the vehicle. We picked up the cases of beer, and proceeded to move toward the party. Now instead of being six crazy Americans wearing sheets in one location, we were six crazy Americans wearing sheets on the move. In the United States, six guys wearing sheets carrying beer on Halloween may not be a big deal, and in a college town, it is pretty much the norm on a Saturday night. But we weren't in a college town, or in the United States. We were in a country where people place a lot of importance on appearance and propriety, and, in case I forgot to mention it, *don't celebrate Halloween.* The final words of the counter-terrorism specialist who gave us our country familiarization brief echoed in my ears: *Don't stand out.*

Finally, after six wrong turns and a brief sprint down an alley to avoid local law enforcement, we arrived at the house. This house would have been pretty big by US standards, so for Spain it was castle. It had seventeen rooms, four bathrooms, four different balconies (with no guardrails, because the Spanish are not nearly as safety conscious as we are), and one of those dining rooms where when people sit on the opposite ends of the table they can hardly hear each other because it is so long. There were marble floors and ornate wooden handrails and exquisite one-of-a-kind paintings. As a guy, my first thought was of course, "Damn, imagine all the chicks I could pick up if I lived *here.*"

It was the perfect place for a Halloween party. It was dimly lit, and a little cold, and it was haunted. Of course, our hosts didn't mention that part until we had all consumed incredible amounts of alcohol, and couldn't operate a doorknob much less a motor vehicle, and as a result were forced to stay there. Later on, we let James sleep in the haunted room, because he was the only one who hooked up at the party, and we were all angry at him anyway.

We were an instant hit when we arrived. Normally, six half-naked men wearing sheets with leaves on their heads might not draw much attention, but we brought beer. Anyway, we turned just about every head when we walked in, and proceeded to mingle and party with the crowd.

The party was a truly international experience. Instead of their just being Spanish women there that we couldn't really communicate with, there were women from Sweden, Norway, France, Italy, and Cleveland, all of whom we couldn't really communicate with. They did all speak the international language of alcohol though, and eventually my friends and I were so intoxicated that we couldn't really communicate with each other much less worry about communicating with folks from different countries.

As the evening progressed, we changed out of our costumes and put on regular clothes. Some members of our group actually were scarier looking in civilian clothes than in their costumes, but fashion sense is somewhat of a rare commodity among my friends.

That party turned out to be the launching platform for much of our social life while in Spain. We met many wonderful people who invited us to several of their parties in hopes that we would show up in their homes wearing bed sheets. Plus, we got some phone numbers of some really cute women that would, at a later date, slap many of us repeatedly. The price we pay for being ambassadors of our great country …

Partying with Man-Hating Women

After our deployment, we returned to the United States. Some time later, we threw our own party. The cast of characters is pretty much the same, minus the international players. Tom still doesn't speak to me.

❦   ❦   ❦

Recently, my roommate and I decided it was time for a party. We didn't really have anything to celebrate, and there were no holidays on the upcoming calendar, but thankfully, our friends didn't care, and all agreed to show up at my house to drink, make loud noises, fall down, and generally act like fools. This differs from when we are in the office, where we usually aren't allowed to drink.

To get ready for the party, we went and bought typical party type food. Chips, dips, soda, beer, those little bite size pizza bagels, more beer, and basically a lot of your general non-healthy items from the party food group. Of course, my roommate never liked to do anything on a small scale, so we went to one of those big bulk warehouse type stores. We bought enough bite size pizza bagels to feed some small African nations, but nothing was too good for our friends.

About an hour before the party started, my roommate asked me what we were going to do to make our party "different." I said she could consider serving Jell-O shooters naked, as she was kind of hot, but that just earned me a quick shot to the ribs and a "Be *serious*." I thought I was. Anyway, at a party we had gone to a few weeks before, one of her friends had purchased an ice sculpture with a hole bored through it. This little invention is called an ice luge, and the idea is you pour a shot of liquor in the top, and put your mouth on the bottom, and an ice cold shot shoots out of the sculpture into your mouth. It was kind of a neat idea, but he had to order it a week in advance, and it cost $200. We didn't have a week, or $200, so we improvised.

God bless America, we actually found a place to deliver a block of ice to our home on short notice. Once it was set up, we used a chain and a crowbar, both heated over the grill, to cut a channel in the ice block. Boom, do it yourself ice luge! We were now ready to have our party.

We began to make bite size pizza bagels, and other appropriate preparations for the party, and in due time our friends began to show up. All was going well, until (drum roll) *enter the cyberstalker.*

I need to back up a bit. I spend a lot of time on the computer, trying very hard not to get run over on the information superhighway, and generally looking at lots of pictures of naked Chinese women. While "online" one night, I met one woman who was "crazy." She would often send me e-mails or instant messages whenever she saw that I was on my computer. Always polite, I would let the conversation drag on until I found some reason to get off the computer—for example, if it was dawn. Through our mostly boring and inane conversations, we found out that we were practically neighbors. She lived two streets over. And then I did something I still to this day don't understand. I mentioned I was having a party, and she should stop by.

Big, *huge* mistake. OK, genius, let's think about this. Here is an unwed mother of four who sent you a picture in which she is not only slightly smaller than Mount Everest, she isn't even *smiling.* She is obviously bitter towards the human race as a whole and the male gender in particular. And I *invited her to my home.* I wish I could say that I was just trying to be nice, and give a woman who doesn't get out much a chance at a little social activity. Truth be told, I was hoping that even if she was a dog, she would bring some cute friends. Most of my friends are male, so we are always looking to increase the number of available members of the fairer sex in our presence. Anyway, I certainly didn't think she would *show up.*

Surprise, enter Broadzilla. She came in, guzzled the drink I made her, and then launched into a male-bashing diatribe that went on for over an hour. I can't even begin to explain how happy I was when more of my friends showed up, allowing me the chance to escape so I could go play host.

I was even happier when Tom arrived. Tom is a great guy, someone who is polite and friendly towards everyone (even bitter man-hating women). I should have been thinking "I should keep Tom away from beast woman." What

I was thinking was "Oh, finally, someone to scrape her off on." Turns out, I didn't have to even work at it. Tom, in his usual nice-to-everyone manner, went up to her just to be nice. She had him trapped for three hours. We actually sent rescue missions in to try and save him.

At one point, I went up to him and said "Tom, that *thing* you wanted to see is in my room," which is not something I was all that comfortable saying to a guy. Tom, because he was trapped behind Bertha the Bitter Behemoth and therefore hadn't had a drink in 90 minutes, caught my drift immediately.

"Oh, the *thing*, yes. You will have to excuse me, I have to go see the thing."

Now Steve, who had consumed plenty of alcohol at this point, also wanted to come see the thing. "Oh, sure, you will show Tom your thing, but not your good buddy Steve. That's cool." He didn't quite get that there *was* no thing, but that we were just trying to break Tom away from the forces of evil that had ensnared him and his good nature.

Well, our plan worked, for a while at least. Some time later, after pushing the limits of how long three men could stay in a bedroom with the door closed, we returned to the party. Tom, ever vigilant for the cyberstalker and *desperately* needing a drink, headed for the bar, poured himself a *very* large class of some fruity, alcoholic substance, and ducked down so he could consume his drink in peace. Also behind the bar was our good buddy James, who knew of Tom's plight, and saw him cowering behind the bar frantically trying to remain out of sight. He also saw Helga the Hideous Hosebeast looking for Tom from across the room.

James didn't hesitate. He sprang into action as a man of only his years and experience could do. He looked at her, looked at Tom, and then back to her, and in a loud, thunderous voice, accompanied by much finger pointing, shouted "*He's over here!*"

Tom, realizing he had been ratted out, immediately sought revenge by dumping his red fruity drink down James' white shirt. James chased Tom out of the house and down the street, and Mammoth Matilda followed at what to her seemed like light speed, losing ground but making up for it by increasing in volume her 14th story about how all men are created in the image of pond scum. We didn't see James for two days, Tom for a week, and, thankfully, Large Marge since.

Just as the trio was dashing out the door, our friend Chris arrived, and with him four *very* attractive women (to this day we don't know how he did it). Forgetting all about Tom and his troubles, the men lined up in order to introduce themselves, use a cheap pick up line, and get shot down. Then we all went back to drinking, along with our new guests. Eventually two of them ended up dancing on my coffee table, and a third was shaking her rump out the living room window. I had to be told all of this in the morning, because my memory from the evening is a bit vague, and also mostly missing.

Apparently, everyone had fun except Tom, whom we have noticed at subsequent parties no longer has such a friendly nature. No one died, and unlike some of our other parties, there were no lawsuits. There was a minor incident when one of my friends got his lip stuck to the ice luge, but that was it. This was cause for celebration, so we immediately planned to have a party, but that's another story …

Attack of the Avocado Woman

As great as my roommate Julia was, she eventually had to move out, and while searching for her replacement, I was inspired to write the following ...

🍁 　 🍁 　 🍁

Recently, my roommate got transferred and had to move out. I was really sorry to see her go. She was intelligent, considerate, neat, cute, smelled good, and generally had all the traits one would look for in a good roommate. Plus, she was nice to me, a quality in short supply among women of today. But duty called, and she had to ship out, leaving behind only memories and her dog, which she could not take with her.

With her gone, and me not wanting to pay the entire rent by myself (that would leave enough money for me to be able to eat dog food for *most* of the month), I began the search for a new roommate.

If you have never tried this yourself, this is not an easy task. You first must advertise that you are looking for a roommate. To do this, you should write an ad that paints an honest picture of what you are looking for. Unfortunately "Rich big-hootered nymphomaniac bimbo wanted to share house with occasionally clean male," while completely upfront and honest, doesn't appeal to too many women, so I had to take a few liberties.

"Female roommate wanted. Must be willing to ignore occasional foul odors. No sex required, but no offer refused."

I had several applicants. Some were actually big enough to be *two* applicants. Once I eliminated those lovelies, plus any applicant wanted for a felony, the pool was pretty slim.

Finally, I found Amanda. She had many of the same traits as my first room-mate and as a bonus, larger breasts. We seemed to get along, and she didn't have a criminal record, so she was well ahead of so many other applicants. We were on course for smooth sailing to happy roommate days, and all was well.

At least until her stuff was delivered. Because she was paying half of the rent, she felt somehow entitled to decorate half the walls. This wouldn't normally be a problem, except that her concept of the word "half" was very close to most people's definition of the word "all." In addition, her taste and mine were only slightly different. The end result was that most of my stuff ended up in one corner of the living room under a blanket.

There were other unforseens as well. I had forgotten that my new roommate hailed from the great state of Texas. Apparently, it is state law that every deco-ration owned by a native Texan must have a cactus, the Texas state flag, or some part of a cow on it. As such, we now have a beautiful (??) glass cactus can-dle holder and the refrigerator is now hidden behind the Lone Star state flag . I do like the steer's horns over the bar, though. She did deviate from the Texas decoration rule with one particular item. She put up a plaque that showed her baby cousin wearing a giant sunflower suit and as a result this blood relation will probably be scarred for life. And she said *my* stuff was tacky.

After the redecoration incidents, things pretty much settled down, and we got along quite well, our tastes in state flags not withstanding. She did have some odd quirks that took some getting used to. For example, she seemed to only take showers when I needed hot water, which resulted in her screaming, which sounded so funny that it resulted in me using even *more* hot water for the sheer entertainment value.

She also had a dog, which she swore was the *smartest* four-legged creature *ever* to walk the earth. Now I admit that I am not much of a dog person, but even so, I had an exceedingly difficult time seeing how this dog was any smarter than the one that I already had in the house. Both smelled funny when wet, ignored me when I called them, and seemed to have to constantly remind themselves what the other's rear end smelled like. Plus, she talked to him in a way that would be sure to turn him into a homosexual dog, even if she hadn't had his testicles lopped off. "Oh, hewwoo you siwee muffin head," she squealed in a high, baby talk sing song voice. I can't be convinced that any dog as smart as she said he was would put up with *that*.

We continued to adjust to each other as roommates. One day, after work, I came out of my room to watch TV. She came out of her room after showering, also to watch TV. At least I found out later that it was her. When she first appeared, she had on a green robe, a green towel on her head, and a *green mask on her face.* I literally jumped when I first saw her. It was like a really bad B-grade movie, *Attack of the Avocado Woman.* We made rules after that incident. In return for me not walking around in my boxer shorts, she agreed not to walk around looking like large members of the squash family.

Occasionally, though, we still had differences of opinion. For example, one Sunday we had some friends over for brunch. Bagels are great brunch-type food, because they don't require much preparation, and also can be rolled across the table for entertainment. I asked Amanda to go purchase some bagels, while I continued to do the manly things required to prepare for Sunday brunch, such as watch football pre-game shows.

Like roommates, bagels can come in several different varieties. Onion, garlic, salt, plain, the list goes on. Most people, when they buy bagels, buy two or three plain ones, and then get some other flavors for variety. Not *my* roommate, though. She bought two dozen bagels, and *every* one was unique. There was not a plain bagel in the bag. We had pesto bagels and tomato bagels and tomato pesto bagels and cheese bagels and raisin bagels and cheese raisin bagels and at least two kinds that had things in them that I could not immediately *recognize*, let alone consider putting in my mouth. Women of the world, if you get nothing else from this story, get this. *It is okay to buy plain bagels.*

Just as we finally got used to all the little quirks of living with each other, it was time for me to move out. I now live by myself, with no Texas treasures, canine marvels, or giant squash. Occasionally, when I see a rather large zucchini, I remember the fun Amanda and I had. In honor of her, I call my neighbor "siwee muffin head" and walk around in my boxer shorts at every opportunity.

"No, Your Honor, I Was Not Stalking Her ..."

What one person may call stalking, another may just call a "really determined effort." You be the judge.

❋   ❋   ❋

Let me start off by saying that I am usually not a stalker. I need to get that out in the open now, so no one thinks that this is my usual method for doing business.

Those of you familiar with my stories might remember my ramblings about a Mr. Chang, and the business trip to Hell that we went on. Well, there was actually one good thing that came out of that trip (well, two; Mr. Chang almost got hit by a bus) that I don't usually mention, because I usually just try desperately to forget Mr. Chang and *all* the time we ever spent together.

While on that trip, I met a girl. Not just any girl, I met *the* girl. She was perfect in every way, at least that I could ascertain while somewhat inebriated. The way it happened was this. The last night of the conference, the hosts put on a Lobster Feast, because the conference was in Maine, and that's how Mainers celebrate everything. At the lobster feast, in addition to watching Mr. Chang struggle mightily with a dead shellfish ("Oh, wat I sposed to du now? How da hewl do I eat dis ding?") I was told by the girl I had been hitting on all week that she lived with her boyfriend. I saw this as a serious speed bump in our relationship, and decided to move on. The problem was that there was no where to move on *to*. The island where we had the lobster feast had absolutely no night life. Actually, there was absolutely no day life either, for that matter.

The local pastime was tide watching. Anyway, without much to do I headed back early.

As I was walking from the pier to the hotel, I noticed noises coming from an alley, and out of sheer boredom decided to investigate. Upon doing so, I found that the entire alley was filled with really small bars. I decided to investigate further, in the interest of both being able to make a complete report and being able to drink a complete beer. As I was walking down the street, two other attendees of the conference took pity on me and my thirst, pulled me into a bar, and bought me a beer. After thanking my gracious companions, I began looking around the bar. I must commend the owner's Maine ingenuity in establishing his tavern. Basically, he put a roof over the alley between two existing buildings, and put a bar across the back. For this he charged a seven dollar cover, but we had nowhere else to go. As we looked around, I couldn't help but notice that the bar was empty. No problem, I had some friends and I had some beer. I was content.

I got a lot more content about an hour later, as after some unknown signal known only to Mainers, beautiful single women by the *dozens* began to arrive. This fact, coupled with the three beers I drank, left me pretty much to the right of ecstatic. As the evening wore on, I began to become less inhibited and even more intoxicated, and thus began to venture out away from our safe table haven to the various corners of the bar, in hopes of bumping into some cutie, spilling my beer on her, and starting a conversation.

On my third such venture, Miss Wonderful, in her oh so sweet voice, asked "OK, how many times are you going to walk past me without saying hello." I fell in love with her somewhere between the words "times" and "are." She was gorgeous. She was witty. She was also blatantly sarcastic, but we'll take the good with the bad in this case. She obviously had guts. This was the woman for me. I wanted to father her children, and get started right there on the spot. Her name was Hanna (no, it wasn't, but I have to protect the guilty) and it was sweet music to my ears.

We got along so well, so fast, it was amazing. We were obviously perfect for each other, and it was a completely perfect evening. At least until the subject of when I was leaving came up. "In sixteen hours" was not what she wanted to hear.

We parted company with a kiss, me knowing no more than her first name, where she went to school, and that she was taking flying lessons: her knowing no more than I was a complete stud, a good kisser, and a NASA test pilot.

For the next week, all I could think about was this girl. I couldn't believe I hadn't even asked for her last name. This was definitely not one of my more crowning social achievements.

I couldn't sleep. I couldn't eat. All I could think about was this girl. I had to find her. Just *had* to, or else I would, well, bother other women, but that was a last resort. How was I going to find her? I didn't know squat about her, and was a few hundred miles away to boot. It wasn't looking good for the home team.

But I didn't give up hope. I called my buddy, Miracle Mike. Miracle Mike was kind of a geek, but he knew more about the internet than any three Japanese guys alive. On top of that, his computer made a Cray Supercomputer look like a Nintendo. Some computer hackers altered bank records. Mike altered planetary orbits. He was *that* good. I explained my situation to him, and told him what I had to work with. He listened intently, told me to bring over his usual fee of a six-pack of beer and some Twizzlers®, and to make sure I wasn't followed.

I arrived at Miracle Mike's and we went to work. We typed in everything we knew and hit "search." We learned lots of interesting things, none of which were really helpful. For one thing, we learned that there are 17 girls with the first name Hanna in Portland, ME. We learned that fifty one people with the first initial of "H" graduated from the school she went to in the three year window I thought she might have graduated. We learned that there were three flight schools in her area offering private lessons. We also learned that some women prefer sex with dogs, but that was an unrelated search.

I went away dejected and morose. How was I ever going to find this absolute goddess? I thought. I thought *hard*. I drank. I drank *hard*. Then, it dawned on me. I needed to start thinking "outside the box," so to speak. More specifically, I needed to start thinking outside the law. I realized that I would never find this absolutely amazing woman if I wasn't daring enough to bend the truth just a bit (more).

Having made this monumental decision, I stopped thinking and started scheming. I called Miracle Mike again, and told him to get me the numbers of those three flight schools in Maine we had found. He obliged, and I sat down, took a deep breath, and loosened up my dialing finger. It was time.

I decided I would call each flight school and pose as a prospective student planning on moving in to the area. During the course of the conversation, I would mention that I heard about their particular program from one of their students. Natural human curiosity would work for me for the first time ever and the school would of course ask *which* student made the recommendation, and I would describe her, and hopefully get her last name.

This is the only time in my whole life that one of my half baked schemes worked anywhere *near* the way it was supposed to. On the very first try, I got a small flight school that put me right through to one of only two instructors on the payroll. I made my pitch, and dropped Hanna's name. "Oh, Hanna Smith?" he asked.

"Yeah, that's it, thanks," I beamed, and of course my next instinct was to slam down the phone. A small voice in my head thought that such an act might raise suspicion, so I refrained. Instead, I got dragged into a forty-five minute sales pitch on the merits of private aviation, for which I was paying about $2.95 a minute long distance.

No matter. When I finally got off the phone, I was ecstatic. I had a last name. With that, it was child's play for Miracle Mike to get an address, and I fired off a letter right away.

The day after I fired off the letter, I got a card from none other than Hanna. Apparently, her intoxicated friend had swiped my business card when I wasn't looking, and she had used that to send me a card at work. As I quickly tore open the envelope, I glanced at the return address. Apparently, Hanna had moved, because the return address was not even close to the address that had cost me the six-pack, Twizzlers, $27.95 in long distance charges, and my integrity to get.

In time our relationship, like all my other relationships, ended, though on the bright side this one ended without gunfire. While she was indeed impressed with my efforts to find her, she was less than impressed with other aspects of my life, like my being hundreds of miles away, and we eventually parted company. I think we both learned a lot from our brief time together. I learned that perseverance and creativity pays off. She learned that two guys with a computer and a bag of Twizzlers should be feared.

Miracle Mike and I have embarked on several other interesting adventures, but I can't make any of them public without getting him in trouble. I can say, however, that he now secretly *owns* the Twizzler company. He has begun to teach me some of his secrets, so that the next time I want to cyber-stalk someone I can do it without his help. Next week I will be taking a business trip to San Diego. We will see what happens.

Dating Dogs and Their Owners

This has happened to me more than just the two times I wrote about below. There are way more women that fall into this category than I originally expected. And as it turns out, I'm now a pretty solid dog person. But at the time, I had a lot to learn …

❋   ❋   ❋

I am 26 years old and single. As such, I am still searching for Miss Right. So far, she eludes me. I have met Miss Right Now, Miss Maybe Later, Miss What Have You Done For Me Lately, Miss High Maintenance, Miss We Can Still Be Friends, and Miss Sorry-I-Slept-With-Your-Best-Friend-Twice-But-I-Couldn't-Help-Myself-Would-You-Still-Be-In-The-Wedding?, but not Miss Right. Having been on the wrong end of so many relationship disasters, I am now unsure of just about everything concerning the future Mrs., except one thing. I am quite sure Miss Right does *not* have a dog.

No, I don't hate dogs. I kind of like them, actually. They can be playful, loving, loyal companions, always there for you no matter how much of a self-centered jerk you happen to be. A dog will remain loyal to you even after you have his testicles removed, which just blows my mind. As many of you know, I have had one testicle removed, and if I *ever* meet up with that doctor …

A dog is very confident in being a dog, and thinks nothing of suddenly stopping whatever it is dogs do and either taking a leak or taking a nap wherever it happens to be. I have trouble deciding which I respect more. Finally, dogs can lick themselves in very intimate places, which is a skill that at one time or another every guy has admired.

So I have no problem with canines. I have no trouble with men who own dogs. I have no trouble with couples who own dogs. I have no trouble with couples who own a couple of dogs. What I do have a problem with is single women who own dogs and expect you to love them as much as they do. I call this the "love me, love my dog" syndrome, and I for one hope they find a cure for it soon, before I go on a dog-shooting rampage.

In my dating disasters, I have met several women who treated their dogs like dogs should be treated, which is to say, like a dog. They fed the dog, they played with the dog, they bathed the dog, but they pretty much kept things in perspective. They did not, for example, spend more time talking to the dog than they did to me. The fact that my relationships with these women did not work out had nothing to do with the dogs, but had to do more with the fact that these women were Satan's daughters, and were spawned rather than born into this world.

The flip side of the coin is the relationships I have had where the dog did indeed come between me and the object of that week's desires. I have changed the names to protect the innocent, which in this case is me.

First was Sandy. Now, I know I said I like dogs, but I didn't mean all dogs. I meant your big, fun loving, playful dogs. Those little annoying Fifi dogs don't count, and I hate them all. Well, Sandy had a Fifi dog, and she spoiled that little bastard rotten. When we cuddled, we *all* had to cuddle. Her, me, and the dog. I had to be fastidiously clean to get anywhere *near* her, but Buddy could have a battalion of fleas on him, and could roll around in cow manure for two days straight and *he* was still allowed in. I won't even discuss flatulence, except to say that I don't know what that damn dog ate, but it should be touted as a "New Source of Natural Gas."

The end of it all came one night when Sandy and I were being, well, *intimate*. As usual, he was allowed to just stay right there in the room and watch the whole show. I fought this on several occasions, but she always threw the "Well, then, you ain't getting' none" card, which as all guys know is pretty much the super-trump of arguments. Anyway, this time Buddy picked a particularly inopportune moment to start licking my foot. I did not really appreciate the attention, as it was distracting me from certain masculine duties. As such, I proceeded to show the little voyeur how much I didn't appreciate his participation by kicking said foot in an attempt to shake him off. I kicked a bit too hard, and by accident sent the little hairy monster into the wall at something like Mach 2. Sandy didn't really appreciate this, and as you can guess, the moment was gone. Soon after that, so was Sandy.

I was able to stay away from dog-women for a while after that, but then I met Brandy. Brandy was a nurse, and she had a dog named Moose. Moose was not a little disposable dog, but actually a good size dog that might have been fun to play with if he wasn't scared of literally everything on the planet. Because I wanted to eventually pet Brandy, I made every effort to pet Moose, and otherwise be nice to him. I even brought him a Christmas present (I gave him a bone. Eventually, I gave one to Brandy too, but that's a different story).

Things were good. Brandy and I were getting along nicely, and Moose and I were playing nicely. Really, the only issue I had was that he slept in her bed, which made it difficult for *me* to sleep there. Like I said, he was a big dog. That coupled with the fact that he left hair on *everything* started to get under my skin after a while, but I endured, because Brandy was pretty cute.

Unfortunately, one night things just went too far, and I snapped. Not only was Moose on the bed, but Cheese, her friend's small, annoying dog, was also there, because Brandy's friend was out of town and Cheese could not possibly survive an entire day without chewing *everything* within eight inches of the ground. As such, when we tried to cuddle, I had to deal with both Moose and Cheese, and that got to be too much. "Look, honey," I said, "I am really just a little tired of trying to avoid having a face full of Cheese's ass, so you need to pick. It's either you sleep with me, or you sleep with the dogs." Well, the dogs are still sleeping there, so you know how that turned out.

With these experiences still very much on my mind (and lots of the dog hair still very much on my clothes), I have decided to pretty much give up on women with dogs. Because I am allergic to cats, I probably won't fare much better with cat lovers. So, this is the plan. I will date either petless women, or women that have harmless, meaningless pets, like turtles, or maybe fish. Women with boa constrictors may also be considered, on a case-by-case basis, because if I married one of them then I could send the boa after those small disposable dogs I hate so much.

Trapper Twins Versus the Skunk

I guess I should thank my parents for providing me an almost endless source of material.

🍁　　　🍁　　　🍁

Growing up in upper middle class suburbia, you can imagine that there weren't a lot of opportunities for my dad to hunt and kill his own food. Don't get me wrong, my dad was several things to our family when we were growing up: a provider, an educator, a warden (that was mostly for my brother). But we were able to get most of our food from conventional upper middle class suburban sources, like the supermarket or the corner store, so Dad's hunting and trapping skills pretty much lay dormant.

Well, with the kids all out of the nest now, Mom and Dad are trying new activities to stave off Alzheimer's. The latest fad is flowers. Lots of them. Enough to outfit two altars at Easter time, at least. And they are literally all over the yard. One Sunday afternoon, the two of them stuck a flower plant in every square inch of dirt that wasn't occupied by some other living organism, and transformed our backyard from a serene and tranquil place of solitude to a botanical garden on steroids.

Mom and Dad were happy with this, but apparently Mother Nature wasn't. As the summer progressed, Mom noticed that some sort of (holy cow, we live in the woods) *animal* was making a four course meal out of her precious Marigolds. Dad immediately took up the cause, and the two of them immediately sacrificed a pachysandra plant and vowed to vanquish this flower-eating scourge from our yard forever.

I love my parents dearly. They are two of the most wonderful people who have ever had the privilege of supporting me. But I have to tell you, when it comes to the outdoors, Trapper John and Buckskin Jane they are *not*. Mom will only go camping if we stay home and do it in the house.

So when our two heroes took on Mother Nature, I knew there would be trouble. Their first attempt involved Dad putting on some surplus fatigues and waiting in the bushes all night for our little flower killer to show up for a midnight snack. Our goldenrod gourmet never showed up, but the mosquitoes did make a meal out of Dad. Mother Nature one, the Trapper twins, zero.

Dad then tried a trap, a big evil pair of spring-loaded steel jaws, which he cleverly disguised as a big evil pair of spring-loaded steel jaws covered with leaves. No animal within seven miles went anywhere near this thing, and the only thing he almost caught was Mom. Mother Nature two, trapper twins, zero.

Two down, and it was late in the ninth (we were almost out of flowers) so Dad dug deep and borrowed another type of trap. This trap was much more humane than the first, as instead of attempting to decapitate the creature, this device merely trapped him so that he may be released into the wild to eat another day. Dad set the trap, and we waited in anxious anticipation …

And then it happened. Dad went outside to check the trap one morning, and low and behold, inside was a skunk. Not just any skunk. This skunk was *huge*. The *king* of skunkdom. This thing was twice the size of our neighbor's dog, and three times as mean as our neighbor. Dad couldn't get within 50 *feet* of the trap without being spotted and odorized by this creature. Nowhere in Dad's book "Trapping for Dummies" was *this* covered.

Mom immediately sprung into action with her favorite weapon, the phone. She began calling pest control specialists up and down the East Coast to find someone somewhere that knew how to handle this situation. Finally, she found Billy Bob's Critter-Be-Gone, and Billy Bob himself said he would rush right over.

When Billy Bob got there, he shrewdly summed up the situation. Here were two outdoors-ily challenged people in a nice house with a trapped skunk. This could only mean one thing: *big* bucks for Billy Bob. He wasted no time in charging my parents $175 dollars to remove said trap, skunk, odor, and all. He then drove down the block, got out of his truck, and released the skunk back into the "wild." This "wild" was approximately 150 yards from where the skunk was caught in the first place.

The skunk, being at this point reasonably *peeved* at having been caught to begin with, and in no way grateful for the limousine ride just received courtesy of Billy Bob, proceeded to head back to our house, bringing reinforcements this time. He and his crew went about happily devouring flowers and stinking up the whole back yard, as my parents looked on in horror. Another point for Mother Nature, and the Trapper Twins still had yet to score.

Mom was tempted to try poison (on Dad) but finally the two compromised and planted plastic flowers. That worked for about a month, until Mother Nature scored again by using the sun to bleach the plastic so that the flowers were all the same faded color of yellow, and looked about as real as Dick Clark's skin.

Winter is coming soon, and Mom and Dad will have the entire season to regroup and figure out how to beat Mother Nature. I love my parents, but I'll give three points and still put money on Mother Nature. Any takers?

On the Importance of Stuff

I'm not really this shallow. I just began thinking one day when I was single how now that I had my own place decorated just the way I wanted, it's time to meet a woman so she can come in and mess the whole thing up. Now that I'm on the other side of that, it was most certainly worth it, but I didn't know that then.

❧　　　❧　　　❧

Let me start by saying that I am *very* single. I mean *very* single. It would be difficult for me to any more single without moving to some deserted island in the middle of the Pacific. Having said this, it is not hard to imagine that my thoughts more and more have turned to finding a mate, so that I do not have to pursue the rest of my life in relationships by myself.

In the absence of having a woman to focus my attentions on, I have taken up several small projects to keep me occupied, such as furnishing a fairly nice home. I actually have real-people furniture, which is significantly different from bachelor furniture, which consists primarily of milk crates. Along with the furniture are some very nice trimmings, like artwork and photographs and the like, all of which I am very attached to. And I'm starting to wonder if that is going to be a problem …

Let's say for argument's sake I meet a young, professional, exceedingly gorgeous woman who is crazy about me, and yes, it *could* happen. She will most likely have her own stuff, just as I have my own stuff. If we fall in love and get engaged, she will want to get rid of *her* stuff and *my* stuff and buy *our* stuff. I am very attached to my stuff, as I have already explained, and therefore would have to break things off in order to preserve my stuff. It really is all about stuff, you see.

The obvious solution to this dilemma is getting a mail order bride. According to almost daily e-mail solicitation, as well as very nice color ads in certain "men's" magazines, lovely women from Latin America *and* Russia are waiting to meet me. For the low cost of something like only five *thousand* dollars, I can fly halfway around the world to look at a veritable line-up of gorgeous women just waiting to marry me. And the best part is *they don't have any stuff!* That's right, no arguments on whether or not we keep my couch, my entertainment center, or my female-leg-in-fishnet-stocking lamp. Plus, the deal comes with a guarantee that we will remain married for at least *two* years, which is probably better than I will do on my own anyway, before she files for divorce and takes half my stuff.

A mail order bride isn't the only option. I could place a personal ad (because I didn't learn my lesson the first time) and specify that I am looking for a stuff-less individual.

Wanted: Gorgeous, intelligent, indigent woman with great body and no belongings. Cannot have strong opinions on interior decorating. Nymphomania a plus.

I could also try and meet women in bars. I could, theoretically, volunteer at the local prison and meet women *behind* bars. I'm pretty sure *they* wouldn't have much stuff.

I guess my best bet is to meet women while shopping. I could go to the stores that carry the kind of stuff that I like, and when I see a woman perusing similar said stuff, I could strike up a pleasant conversation and just go from there. Our conversation would turn from stuff to each other and soon we could be madly in love. Years and years of marital bliss with someone who has the same tastes as I do.

Hmmmm.

On second thought, there is something to be said for variety …

Diane Dated My Clone, and Boy, Did That Bug Me

Mixed reviews on this one. Most people like it, with the exception of my parents, who thought it contained more than the usual amount of pain (it does) and the wonderful woman who inspired Diane, who thought some of my comments were just a little too pointed (she's quick, I'll give her that). I didn't write it for any other reason than to vent some of the frustration I was feeling over the entire situation. "Diane" and I stayed friends for a little while, and sometimes I wondered if there weren't more chapters to write in the story of our relationship, but it was not to be. You will find some of my stories funnier, but none of them more true. This one hurt, but that's what made it worth writing.

※   ※   ※

You are never going to believe this, but finally, after much searching, I met her. Not just any her. *Her.* The *one.* The one I had been waiting, praying, longing, searching, and sacrificing small animals for. The one I almost spent five thousand dollars to fly to Russia and find. *That* one.

I didn't realize it right away. The first time I met her, I noticed she was attractive, and had a pretty smile, and that she was walking away from me. No big deal. After all, lots of women walk away from me, and I'm fairly used to it. But through work we ended up as acquaintances, then we met for lunch a few times, then once for dinner, and then *wham* I was singing love songs from the eighties and generally acting goofy all the time.

Her name was Diane. And no, she wasn't perfect. She ate too much, and she never covered her mouth when she yawned. But the rest of her was so amazingly *cool* that these little imperfections only made me want to be with her *more*. She was intelligent and funny and caring and spiritual and deep and (by the way) 6 feet tall, and blond, and amazingly beautiful, and athletic and ... well, enough already. Basically, she was everything I ever thought to ask for in a woman, with some cool extras thrown in at no charge. She had a better jump shot than I did, for one.

Being with her caused me to do all sorts of really dumb things. One night we were in the car returning from a party, and I somehow tricked her into letting me hold her hand. She passed dreamily into a light sleep, and I just drove and listened to the radio and held her hand and all was right with the world. As I continued along happily, I started to get a little warmer. Thinking it was just the pleasure of her company, I paid it no mind. But then, as it went from warm to warmer to bloody *hot*, I realized that the only way to avoid being roasted alive would be to turn down the heater. *That* would require me to either let go of her hand, or let go of the steering wheel. Letting go of the steering wheel would mean loss of control, a head on impact, and possibly death. Letting go of her hand seemed way worse. So, I refused to do either, and as a result created an atmosphere similar to Hell in July just so I wouldn't have to let go of her fingers.

It didn't stop there. I found myself doing things with her that I would never *ever* do in a normal, loveless state of mind. Unexplainable things, like going to Pottery Barn. Yes, Pottery Barn. For those of you men who know what Pottery Barn is, I promise not to tell anyone, but you should still feel ashamed. For those who don't (and I congratulate you) I will explain. Picture a store that is about 180 degrees off of any store a man would want to go into. Pottery Barn is one step shy of that. But there I was, on a Sunday afternoon, no less, buying a giant metal X and a giant metal O. The reasoning escapes me, except that she smiled at me when she asked if I liked them, and I was a *complete* sucker for her smile. Every time she smiled at me, my heart dove into my toes and my Adam's apple shot to the top of my skull. I also usually experienced difficulty speaking, and often blushed for the next twenty minutes. Occasionally, I drooled.

Despite these difficulties, things were great, and I was beyond happy. We went out. We laughed. We connected. We had *conversations*. Real ones, that didn't involve cars or football. We *talked*. Like about family and dreams and life experiences and stuff that I would *never* bring up with the guys. We spent a whole day together and didn't discuss sports *once*. I haven't done that since June 11, 1993, and I was unconscious that day. In addition, I discovered that I actually had *real* feelings towards her. Important ones. Ones that didn't involve her removing her shirt. This was definitely new ground for me, and while I didn't know where exactly this was all headed, I was really enjoying the trip.

Of course, behind such a great buildup, there looms an imminent cloud of disaster. One day, after much soul searching, I poured my heart out to her, and told her everything I was feeling. She listened intently, and then told me how *close* she felt to me (which was good). So *very* close to me (which was even better). And how much fun she had with me, and how comfortable she was around me (more good things). And how it felt (picture me on the absolute edge of my seat, waiting to hear what comes next) like I was her ... *brother.*

Ouch, and by "ouch" I mean that in the sense of "sucking chest wound." For those of you from West Virginia, "brother" is bad, at least when used to describe *you* by a woman *you* are trying to trick into falling in love with *you.*

If it had stopped there, things would have been fine. I have a varsity letter in being rejected, and could have handled it fairly easily. But God wasn't done with me yet, so it got worse. Because she was such an amazing person (and really hot besides) I decided that just being in her general vicinity was better than not being around her at all, and we remained friends. It was difficult, but I managed to veil the fact that I pretty much wanted to marry her the next time both of us had a free moment, and things were tolerable for a while.

And then she told me she met someone. Not just any someone, but someone *special,* someone she wanted to spend more time with. As she was my friend, at least part of me was happy for her. Admittedly, it was a small part. The other, larger part of me wanted to kill him, but that's the Sicilian in me.

Like a good friend, I asked questions about him (know your enemies ...).

He was Italian (I've been Italian my whole life) and he was Catholic (I've been Catholic my whole life, too) and he was an engineer (and *surprise* so was I. As it turns out, we were both even *aerospace* engineers, which was even scarier.). She even showed me a picture, and I'll be a damned if we didn't *look* alike. He did have more hair than me, and was taller, but I dress *way* better, so I counted that as a draw. Bottom line, she didn't want *me,* but apparently dating someone just *like* me was not only acceptable, it was preferable to the real thing. Except for the height difference, she was practically dating my clone. How does *that* work?

I tried to play it off like it didn't bother me, but I failed. There should be a rule against this sort of thing. No dating anyone like the last person you rejected for at least sixty days. I finally couldn't take it anymore, and just had to ask her. "What does he have that I don't?" She thought. She squinted up her eyes and thought *hard* (she was blonde, after all). Finally, she came up with a pretty good answer. "Well," she cooed with an embarrassed smile, "*me*."

Things in our relationship have pretty much settled down since then, and we are both comfortable in our roles. Diane's role is to date guys that don't deserve her and don't treat her as well as I would (because they aren't me), while continuing to convince herself (and me) that there will never be anything between us. My role is to hide my feelings behind a façade of friendship while dating women who don't make me feel half as goofy as Diane does (because they aren't Diane). Occasionally, we get together to discuss how we are both "OK," but that we haven't met that "special someone."

I won't pray that God moves her heart so that we could be together. That's a lot to ask. I guess I can only pray that she meets someone who would treat her like I would, and that I meet someone that makes me feel like she does, without the drooling, of course.

I also pray that *she* has a clone, but that may be a stretch, too …

The Return of the Amazing Amanda

Another story about my friend Amanda. Believe it or not, I miss living with her ...

✻   ✻   ✻

You might remember my old roommate Amanda from an earlier story ("Attack of the Avocado Woman"). Well, bless her heart, she came to visit me last weekend. It was great to see her, we got to catch up, and of course having her around reminded me of all the things that I used to pick on her for when we were roommates.

Within five minutes of her arrival into the guest room, the place was a disaster. It literally looked like an underwear bomb had gone off. She was visiting for five days, and apparently brought enough underwear to change every 33 seconds for the duration of her trip. I've been in department stores that didn't have this much underwear. It was *everywhere*. On the bed, on the floor, on the mirror, hanging from the ceiling fan, on the doorknobs, hanging on the lamp. It was beyond words.

Not that, as a single man who spends significant effort trying to view female underwear, I was complaining. I was just making an observation.

Now, one would think that with so much underwear to choose from, it would be fairly east to find a suitable pair. Therefore, one would not expect Amazing Amanda to take longer than one calendar month, at the absolute maximum, to get ready to go out to dinner. So, seeing that she was out of the shower and getting changed, I went downstairs to wait for her. I waited. And waited. And watched the second half of a football game. And waited some more.

And finally, when I could stand it no longer, I went upstairs to find out what in the heck was taking her sooooooo long. I knocked on the door, and she opened it just a crack, and I politely asked what in bloody blazes what taking so long. And she looked me straight in the eye and said, "I can't find any underwear."

I was floored. I was shocked. I was so beside myself it was like I had a twin brother. After my recovery, I politely but loudly pointed out that there was approximately seventy-seven *pairs* of lacy woman's underwear strewn all over the room, and could she please just pick *one* so we could eat dinner sometime before breakfast?

At that point, she began to give me what can only be defined as "panty education." As she explained it to me, none of the underwear that was strewn about like so much confetti was acceptable for wear beneath her slacks, because *all* of them would show "panty lines." So, she was looking for her thong. Apparently, despite bringing what could only be described as *truckloads* of underwear to my home, she indeed only brought *one* thong, and was searching through the multitudes of cotton, lace and whatever else they make female unmentionables out of to find it. She thought she was getting close, though. In the hour since she had started looking she had worked her way across half the room, and only had the other half to get through before we could leave.

I gave up. I went downstairs to make myself a sandwich and watch the second half of some Kevin Costner epic. Finally, as it was ending, I hear the lovely Miss Amanda call downstairs. I dared hope that maybe we were *finally* going to leave the house before I paid off my mortgage …

Sadly, it was not to be. The search for the thong had been fruitless, and we were now on plan b. She asked me if she could borrow a pair of my boxers, which I produced in about thirty seconds. She happily accepted them, and then spent the next thirty minutes looking for a matching bra (which I am happy to say I could *not* provide).

We never did make it to dinner that night. She promised to make it up to me the next morning by taking me to breakfast. I got up at 8, waited for her to pick out some shoes, and finally made it to breakfast by one o'clock that afternoon.

At least she let me pick the restaurant.

Christmas, as Seen From Low Earth Orbit

This one has always been pretty popular, and a few friends have asked me to send it to their families during the holidays, which I find incredibly flattering. This one I have to dedicate to my dad. He just takes Christmas to a whole different level.

❄   ❄   ❄

My father was the seventh child of eight, and as such was never able to get near the bathroom until his older sisters went to college. That of course has nothing to do with the fact that his father was a retail food merchant, and was very busy around Christmas time. Because of that, Christmas in his house was always pretty hectic, and there was never time for decorating or tree trimming or anything like that. My father vowed that when he had a family, he was going to make up for lost time. Christmas was going to be the high point of the year, every year, for the rest of his life, and his family was going to have a jolly holiday, dammit, even if it killed us. And a couple times, it almost did.

Things didn't start off out of control. My family's Christmas decorations had a rather humble beginning, actually. That first year, Dad put up a wreath and Mom put up a tree, and things were pretty much low key that season. Then I was born, and as I grew, so did Dad's commitment to having the house visible from orbiting spacecraft.

I remember helping my parents decorate the house when I was first growing up. Dad, with my "help" (I was in charge of drinking hot chocolate), would put up about seven hundred colored lights around our front door and windows. As this was the seventies, and things like energy conservation, electrical safety, and good taste hadn't been invented yet, these were not the cute, soft, little twinkle lights so popular today. No sir, these were the gaudy, power guzzling two-inch long behemoths of yesteryear. They came about six to a strand, and when we plugged them in, the rest of the lights in the neighborhood would dim. After about an hour these things put out enough heat to melt the polar icecaps. We also wrapped the front door in tin foil, and put a large wreath up on the side of the house, so that everyone knew that we knew it was Christmas.

The inside of the house was Mom's domain, though she did allow Dad to come in from time to time. For about three weeks prior to Christmas, Mom would unpack decorations and put up little candles and bows and Santas and a whole bunch of other things. Mom did allow Dad and I (again, I mostly drank hot chocolate) to decorate the trees, and I do mean plural. As long as I can remember, my family has always put up two trees. The one in the living room was fake, but we always said either "artificial" or "living impaired" so as not to hurt its feelings. It was decorated in a very formal manner, just green and gold. No red anywhere in sight, and Mom strictly enforced that. I tried to hang a red ball on it once, and got spanked with a giant candy cane. Now *that's* the true meaning of Christmas. Green and gold, no questions, no exceptions. Santa was watching.

Our second tree was a real tree, downstairs in the basement. In keeping with Dad's theme of putting lights on everything within reach, this tree was covered with colored lights. These were the indoor version of the ones outside, slightly smaller and less kilowatt consuming. Still, my family's holiday energy use contributed heavily to this country's race to perfect nuclear power. They also produced slightly less heat, but were every bit as gaudy. In addition, we put lots of brightly colored glass balls on the tree, in order to cover the tackiness of the lights with an even greater tackiness. Still, this was the seventies, and tacky was in, so we were happy.

Downstairs across from the tree is where we set up the manger scene. A manger scene, for you pagans, is a depiction of the birth scene of the baby Jesus. A typical manger scene has the Holy Family, an angel, two shepherds, three kings, and animals commonly found in the Middle Eastern region, such as sheep and donkeys and oxen. Our manger scene, which took up most of the basement, had the extended Holy Family, including aunts and uncles, four shepherds, an entire flock of sheep, six oxen, two donkeys, about a battalion of angels (not the cute little cherubs, either), the three kings with their queens and concubines and bodyguards and camels, and a whitetail deer. Yes, one whitetail deer. Not being very smart, I never realized that whitetail deer do not normally inhabit the Middle Eastern regions. Apparently, Dad's little sister gave it to him, and made him in a moment of weakness promise to make it a part of our manger scene, and zoological propriety be damned. Mom has often since been grateful that Dad did not have a younger brother who gave my father a model car, or else the manger scene might contain Joseph and Mary in a '57 Chevy (though I always thought that would look really cool).

As I got older, our decorative scheme became rote. We went to extremes every year, but it was the same extreme, so we were comfortable, and a little bored. Then one day, my brother was born, even though I had asked Santa for a puppy, and we had to move. My entire twelve years of life were turned upside down, and just when I thought things couldn't get any worse, here comes Christmas.

Our new home presented some interesting decorating challenges. It had an entire extra section of roof to decorate, for one thing. For another, it was a lot longer, and if we were to continue to use the seventies lights, which in the eighties were getting expensive, my parents would have to get another mortgage. Finally, there was an entire new power grid to tamper with.

Our first attempt in the new home was a valiant effort, but extremely inefficient. In order to get all the lights to go on, we had to throw two switches, plug in six plugs, and fire up an auxiliary generator. But everything looked great, and we vowed to better ourselves in the coming seasons.

As the years progressed, we learned from our mistakes, and every year we made improvements in the system. Our triumph came the Christmas of my senior year in college. On that blessed occasion, after studying electrical diagrams for three weeks prior, and spending $312 on extension cords and those little things you screw into light sockets so you can plug said extension cords into them, we were able to get all of our holiday decorations to light up from only *two* switches. We celebrated. Then we sang. Then we blew two fuses in our house, and one across the street. We have several times since tried to get everything to run off just one switch, but sadly the goal still eludes us. One year, after a particularly bad start, we actually regressed to three. Dad took that pretty hard, but he's OK now.

Coming from a large Italian family (meaning that it is a family of very large Italians) no discussion of the holiday season would be complete without discussing food. Christmas Eve dinner is perhaps the most joyous meal in my family, and every year we prepare for it with the same zeal that the Allies prepared for Normandy (it's about that noisy, too.). Each year we alternate between our brightly decorated house and my dad's cousin's house. Their house is about the same as ours, except, according to them, more "tastefully" decorated, which is the polite way of saying they put up a lot less lights. We invite all the relatives in the local area in for the feast.

And what a feast it is! The traditional Italian Christmas Eve dinner includes seven different kinds of fish. The traditional Italian Christmas Eve dinner in my family also includes six different kinds of pasta, five different types of pastries, four bottles of wine (per person), three types of scotch, two turtle doves, and a Frank Sinatra Christmas album.

As we gather around the table stuffing ourselves, the older members of the family engage in the timeless family tradition of getting hammered, coupled with the other timeless family tradition of getting really *loud*. As they do this, Mom always picks this time to break out the video camera to record the event. As Mom has often had a few drinks herself, her ability to hold the camera steady is somewhat disrupted. The end result every year is a ten minute long movie of a bunch of older drunk people yelling loudly at the sober grandchildren during what appears to be an earthquake.

And honestly, I wouldn't trade any of it.

How to Steal a Naked Woman

It's funny what a few years will do to your opinions about naked women. When I was younger, I put more effort into stealing a Playboy *than I have into some of my much more recent relationships. Maybe that's why the* Playboys *are still here ...*

❀　　　❀　　　❀

Lots of guy's dads have collections. Collections they don't really want their young sons with their grubby hands and grubby friends playing with. One of my friend's fathers collected antique cars. We were, on special occasions, allowed to get near enough to recognize that they were indeed ground vehicles, and on even rarer occasions to determine the color. Another friend's father collected firearms, and a third collected antique edged weapons. Or so I had been told, because we never were allowed anywhere near those collections. This was probably a wise practice, as with access to such arsenals we would immediately have declared war on the adjoining neighborhoods.

My dad had them all beat, and I was the envy of all my friends, at least through our early teen years. My dad had the ultimate collection, according to the tastes of just-recently-post-pubescent boys. My dad collected the ultimate icon of male-ism, that esteemed publication, the one, the only, *Playboy.*

My dad was good at many things. He was a great father, and in addition could build really cool things in the garage. He applied this same zeal to his collecting, and as such, had the *complete Playboy* collection, right up to whatever month it happened to be at the time. This of course made him, and by association *me*, very popular with my friends.

Young teenage boys will spare no effort in trying to see the naked female form, and we were no exception. One of my buddies put forth a little *too* much effort, and got himself arrested and his binoculars impounded, but we did learn from that mistake, and refocused our efforts towards seeing the naked female form on paper instead. Our next step was to actually obtain the paper with the naked female form on it.

We approached the situation the same way that generals approach major military campaigns. As the leader, I first stated the objectives. "Men, today we are going to see a naked woman." I then would outline the risks, which included the environment (the magazines were kept in the attic and the garage, which were dirty), roving patrols (my sister and her friends), the enemy leadership (that would be Mom), and the possibility of imprisonment (grounding) if caught.

We would perform reconnaissance, going into the garage or the attic to "fetch a rake" or "check on the Christmas decorations." One time, I actually said I was looking for one of my old third-grade textbooks.

Reconnaissance complete, we would move to the next phase. Lookouts would take position in the living room, the base of the driveway, and out in front of the garage. This team in place, the actual extraction team would move in, and ever so gently lift the cover off of whatever box we hoped contained our prize (a *Playboy* usually almost as old as we were, because the current issues were never kept in the garage). As the cover came off, we would let out a heavy sigh at the stapled volumes of naked, smiling women before us. We couldn't linger long, though, so we quickly made a selection and removed it gingerly from the box, replacing the cover like the best of cat burglars. Off we scurried to one of our rooms, and recalled the lookout team. We would now spend hours "reading the articles" and discussing in detail how what was between the pages inspired us.

I have many fond memories of those episodes. And a few not-so-fond ones, like when a lookout was distracted by my sister's pretty friend, so my sister showed up in the garage just as the box cover was coming off. That was a little tricky to explain, and in the end I had to bribe her with two weeks' allowance, *plus* a promise to be nice to her, and sometimes I'm *still* afraid she will tell Mom.

That was then, this is now. The *now* is that I'm old enough to buy my own *Playboy*, and I almost never do. Recently, Dad approached me and asked me to use the internet to help sell off the duplicates of his collection (on the information superhighway, Dad is that annoying guy who drives 45 in the passing lane). Now, where I used to spend hours trying to obtain *one Playboy*, I now spend hours trying to get rid of *dozens* of *Playboys*. Serves me right, I guess.

On the other hand, when is the next time I will have so many naked women at my place?

How the Pyramids Were Built

Meet my dad, the home improvement guru. This story is easy to prove. There is 650 feet of evidence surrounding my parents' house.

❦   ❦   ❦

My father was a home improvement visionary. He had the incredible ability to think years into the future when it came to projects around the house, and they were *never* small in scale. Nothing he ever planned, not a single project, ever lasted less than six months. Two of them have been going on longer than my brother has been alive. My brother drives now.

Having been exposed to this for my entire life, even I was surprised one day when Dad took me outside and pointed to his latest creation. There before me stood a small, modest rock wall. It was about three feet high, a foot wide, and ten feet long. Dad was very proud of his wall, and I tried to look impressed, so as not to hurt his feelings. "See what I did in just twenty minutes?" he happily boasted. "I want to do this around the entire yard." Well, even at 14 years old I knew that this meant "I want *us* to do this around the entire yard." Dad proceeded to tell me that we needed to begin gathering rocks. My sister would gather twenty-five a day. I would gather fifty, as I was older, stronger, and more deserving of punishment because I was born first. Using "Dad math" (which is not based on "real math"), he estimated we would be able to surround our acre and a half property by early the following spring. And so began an engineering marvel not seen since Egyptian fathers conned Egyptian children into building the pyramids.

We dutifully began gathering rocks every day of the week. It quickly became evident that we were not gathering enough rocks, because three weeks later the wall was still not done. Dad increased mine and my sister's quota to 75 and 50 rocks, respectively. That lasted a week. Then it was 100 and 60. Two weeks later I was gathering 125, and she was pulling up 75. At this point we formed a union, and went on strike until better working conditions were offered. The gracious offer from management was an extra dollar a week allowance, we could continue to eat, and Dad might forget about the rebellion before I learned to drive and needed the car. We came to terms, and production resumed.

Dad would do actual wall construction on the weekends, using up the rocks piled during the week. We would continue to gather rocks, while Dad would stack. Now, in the beginning, Dad was not an expert on rock wall building (though he did eventually achieve that status). There were several collapses, a few avalanches, and twice we had to suspend operations in order to dig out various members of the family. On the bright side, we kids learned a whole bunch of really cool words that we were never supposed to use. Dad eventually got very good at stacking rocks, and I quickly began my apprenticeship in the delicate field. As we got better, we discovered that the initial segments of the wall were doomed to collapse, and Dad improved upon the design. We moved on, our spirits bolstered by the fact that we were now constructing a quality product destined to last longer than the Mayan temples. And ours wouldn't be full of dead people, either.

The final dimensions of the improved segments were four feet high, and two feet thick at the base. It took about thirty rocks to do one linear foot of wall, big rocks on the bottom and smaller rocks at the top. This wall can stop tracked vehicles. I am proud to say that my parents own the only house in the neighborhood reasonably secure from armored assault. Finally, after three *years*, we had surrounded the entire property, and Dad began planning our next project.

The experience would be painful enough if it ended there, but of course it didn't. I mentioned that Dad got *very* good at stacking rocks, but he only did this through practice, *lots* of practice. The last 350 feet of the wall will be here long after my grandchildren are running their own crime families. However, the first 300 feet were, well, a warm-up. This meant that I spent the next two years repairing the parts of the wall we built the first two years. This meant that *I* got real good at stacking rocks. A useful skill, but one that I seldom use in my career as an aeronautical engineer.

In the end, I am glad we took on this project. Whenever I go home, I look with pride on our accomplishment. It did so much for our family. It made my dad happy. It did wonders for my upper body strength. It kept the neighbors away. Out of a desire to have my own similar bonding experience with my children and also out of revenge, I have already begun planning a similar project for my as yet un-purchased home. I have had several ideas, but none meet the dual requirements of taking longer than five years plus having a high likelihood of broken bones.

Maybe I will ask Dad for suggestions.

Shopping is Not an Olympic Sport

This story was inspired by too many trips to the mall with my mom, my sister, and a slew of other women who viewed shopping as an all-day event.

❋　　　❋　　　❋

To everyone (except maybe my cousin Vern, who has never even spoken to a woman in his life and wouldn't know) it is pretty obvious that God created men and women differently. At no time is this more apparent than in the shower.

Because, however, this is a family oriented story, I will not write about those obvious differences, but instead discuss the differences between the shopping habits of men and women. I realize that many of the women in the audience are saying to themselves, "Well, this ought to be short. Men don't *have* shopping habits." Ha, prepare, naysayers, to be educated.

Men do indeed have shopping habits. They are just less apparent than that of the fairer sex, because we don't practice them every waking moment that we are not at work or fixing our hair.

Men have a completely different mentality when it comes to shopping. I will not evoke the stereotype that women spend more money than men. Not true. The difference is the time factor. If a man and a woman are each given $1500 to spend on clothing, the woman will take approximately two presidential terms to decide which size blazer and matching slacks she wants, while the man will buy the first thing that fits, provided it is sold to him by an attractive female sales clerk, and matches something in his closet that he is at least fairly certain he still owns.

Shopping for men is not a social activity. It is a mission. We plan; we prepare; we execute. We walk into the store, go straight to the section of the store which contains what we need (or to women's underwear, as a diversion). We pick up our items, we pay, we leave. If two men are shopping, the conversation is strictly mission essential, resembling cockpit tapes from jet fighter dogfights.

FIRST GUY: "Red two, this is red leader. Break off and acquire pair of pants. Over"

SECOND GUY: "Wow, look at the knockers on that sales clerk! I am engaging, over."

Shopping for women, on the other hand, is a social event. It is to be attended by many, and the only requirement is that a good time is had by all. Accomplishing anything of real value, at least by guy standards, is secondary. It is perfectly acceptable for a pack of women to go shopping all day, try on 3,461 different outfits, and buy nothing more than a box of tic-tacs.

That is why there is seldom seen a more miserable creature than a man shopping with a woman. He wants to stop in two places, and they both sell *Playboy*. She wants to stop everywhere else. *Everywhere* else. Whether or not the store is selling something the woman needs doesn't matter. The store could be selling accessories for the well-dressed trans-sexual amputee on the go, and the woman will need to go inside. "I just need to check something real quick," she explains. Two hours later, she has bought a nicely shaved wooden leg, with a set of stockings, and now *you* have to carry them throughout the mall for the rest of the day.

This is why I intend to create a shopping mall totally for guys. Wide aisles, guy music, one small clothing store, seven stores devoted to sports, two more to cars, and Hooters' girls at the checkouts. Complimentary beer when you walk in. No stores selling anything French. Now *that's* a mall where I could spend a Saturday afternoon.

You Will Defend Your Asparagus

Another girlfriend story, but one involving a different girlfriend; the first of two inspired by this particular lady.

❋   ❋   ❋

My girlfriend and a friend of hers have a p-patch. I'll explain what that is, before the perverts in my audience get an image of an outdoor litter box for women. Basically, it's a small patch of land they rent from a farmer so they can have a garden. It's for people who want to garden but are handicapped by living in a condo or a house with dog that chews everything.

Anyway, their patch is right in the middle of about twenty other patches, all being farmed by various different people in various different ways, a patchwork sort of garden. Some people grow flowers; some grow vegetables, some fruits, whatever strikes them as needing to be grown.

Along with working the patch, these part-time farmers must learn "patch etiquette," which is largely based on the honor system. It involves simple things we all should have learned growing up. Don't take what isn't yours, don't reap what you didn't sow, don't drag your garden hose through someone else's tomato plants, that sort of thing. People leave their gardening equipment, hoses, tools, and seeds out in the open, and trust that no one will disturb these tools, and therefore all live in harmony.

I was a first hand witness to this etiquette, as I was drafted into going with my girlfriend one afternoon to water her garden. "C'mon, it will be fun," she lied. She spent the next hour watering and weeding and planting and working. I spent the next hour whining and moaning and drinking and burping, but that's not important. What is important was that she dutifully observed patch etiquette, and did not disturb any of her neighbors' tools. Other people were working their patches, and they did not disturb any of their neighbors' tools either, and all were in harmony when we left.

Or so we thought. When we returned a few days later, we noticed that all the zucchini leaves were torn off on one side of the patch. She thought that was sort of strange, but that maybe her friend did it for some undisclosed reason. Well, it turns out her friend *didn't* do it, so they could only surmise that their "neighbors" in the adjacent patch were upset because the leaves encroached onto their "property." And so they took matters into their own hands and removed the offending leaves.

I immediately planned wholesale retaliation (that's the Sicilian in me coming out) but my girlfriend, a much more level-headed sort, decided to politely confront the neighbors at the earliest opportunity, which turned out to be the next day. They grudgingly apologized, and presented a peace offering of asparagus, which was graciously accepted by my girlfriend and later messily devoured by me.

We left, thinking all was right with the gardening world. Not so. Somewhere between when we left and the next day, war was declared. It started out innocently enough. Apparently, one p-patch farmer needed to borrow another p-patch farmer's hose, and because the second farmer wasn't available to either grant or deny permission, the first farmer took matters into her own hands and borrowed the hose. This worked great, until the second farmer returned, and immediately was upset with the first farmer for borrowing the apparently-cherished aforementioned hose. Words were exchanged, the hose was returned, feathers smoothed, and life continued.

Until the first farmer left, at which point the second farmer, in retaliation, "borrowed" some of the first farmer's artichokes, or so he thought. In reality, he "borrowed" some totally un-involved farmer's artichokes, who now had no choice but to seek retribution that evening by kidnapping and summarily executing two watermelons and a squash, leaving the entrails strewn about the offending farmer's patch.

The following day several "incidents" occurred, with vegetables being kidnapped, fruit being assaulted and bruised, and even a beheading (of a lettuce plant).

In the following week, things quickly escalated from there, both in the numbers of vengeful part-time farmers involved and the level of violence born by the grown produce. I think the police became involved when two tomato plants were doused in gasoline and torched. The retaliation, which involved unnatural things done to zucchini, also warranted police attention. The entire thing came to a head when one farmer, obviously well read, re-enacted the salting of Carthaginian fields by the victorious Romans, ensuring that his neighbor's patch wouldn't yield anything except dirt for the foreseeable future.

My girlfriend, while not an active participant in the mayhem, did spend countless hours defending her patch from the rioting and looting that quickly consumed the whole of that small farm. She could often be seen, hoe in hand and bucket on her head, behind a small fortress made of topsoil bags, defending her honor and her strawberries. I was never so proud.

This war, as wars tend to do, finally ended, but only after massive casualties on all sides. The carnage was unbelievable. Crushed tomatoes, trampled beets, melons dismembered by left-over fireworks. The number of pea pods killed was well into the hundreds.

The conflict had a profound effect on my girlfriend. She retired forever from the world of gardening, choosing to leave it to the professionals, and the non-psychotically aggressive. Having hung up her hoe, she has planned to start a much more genteel hobby.

Roller derby starts next week.

My Broken Heart

Yet another of my little health "hiccups," not nearly as bad as the first, but scary in its own way.

❦   ❦   ❦

I ran into another health problem recently. Seems my heart doesn't quite work right. The doctors think they can fix it, and assured me that even if they can't, not to worry, because they still get paid.

Everyone knows, or should know, that the heart has four chambers. Two aortas, two ventricles, with a left and right for each. These have to contract in a specific order, or else, basically, you die, or else at least are *really* uncomfortable. The chambers are told when to beat by electronic impulses coming from what's called an SA Node (and no, I don't remember what SA stands for, so let it go). Picture the chambers as workers, and the SA Node as the foreman. Well, in my case, the foreman is drunk or crazy, because the chambers don't always beat in the right order, and the end result is I'm either exhausted by walking up stairs, or else have a heart rate that feels like it's somewhere in the neighborhood of 1000 beats per minute.

In order to correct this condition, the doctors first tried medicine, which made me grumpy, sleepy, lethargic, irritable, and foggy. Because I'm usually not sleepy, people could tell something was amiss, and I went to see another doctor.

This doctor wanted to try what he called a "routine procedure." This "routine procedure" involved sticking electrodes into my heart via three of my four major arteries. How this is "routine" is beyond me. I have spent a good part of the 31 years of my life trying *not* to get things stuck into my heart or *any* of my arteries, and this sudden departure from that so-far-successful practice disturbed me. Further, I totally agree with my good friend David, who succinctly observed that "It's only routine when it happens to someone else."

Anyway, the doctor didn't give me much choice (I guess he needed to make a quota or something for the month), so off to the operating room I went. Before surgery I had to sign a waiver which said something along the lines of "Due to the nature of this procedure, the following may occur: Infection, disease, bleeding, blood disorders, scars, and oh-by-the-way death." Basically, anything greater than a hangnail was not their responsibility. Again, this was all "routine," but by this point, that didn't really fill me with a whole lot of confidence.

I arrived at the hospital early in the morning, and just like my other surgeries (it's an expensive hobby) was immediately put into a hospital gown which left nothing to the imagination. This time however there was the added fashion statement of disposable booties, so that I could better walk around and display my wares in the above hospital gown. I decided to lay low on the plywood sheet that passed for a bed until it was time to go.

The actual procedure involved forcing electrodes upstream through my arteries into my heart, then observing which electrical nodes were doing what. Upon establishing the baseline, Doctor Jekyll would then apply "electrical impulses," which is a nice way of saying "shocks," to my heart in hopes of getting it to misbehave in the operating room the same way it does virtually ever other day when I'm *not* in the operating room.

We've all heard that the way to a man's heart is through his stomach, so imagine my surprise when I learned that the arteries to be used for cardio access weren't exactly in my stomach. Two were in my groin, and the third (because there were no more available arteries in my groin) was in my neck. So the gist of the procedure was that one stranger in the operating room administered my drugs while another shaved my groin and neck, and a third cut little holes in me to route electrodes through. I've had better days.

Things got pretty hazy after that. I don't really remember much of the procedure, and I woke up as they were wheeling me back to the recovery area. Once in the recovery area, they pumped me full of fluids, and then made sure I understood that I could not move my lower body for the next six hours. This was necessary, because the doctor wasn't real sure he had sewn up my groin properly, and the hospital didn't want to pay the custodians overtime if I sprung a leak and bled all over the floor.

Three hours into my six hours of mandatory non-movement, all those fluids that the wonderful hospital staff had put *in* now wanted to come *out*. Of course, any possible voiding of my bladder would involve movement of my currently immobile lower body, which was strictly off limits, because providing bladder relief could also involve my death. This was to be avoided, because it could result in excessive paperwork for the staff, and it was near the end of the work day. Therefore, I needed to hold it for the next three hours as my legs healed up. You know you are having a bad day when your sole purpose for the day, the thing you are looking forward to most, is peeing.

Finally, after an excruciatingly loooooong wait, I was allowed to go to the bathroom, which resulted in one of the most glorious acts of urination I have ever experienced. Upon completion, I promptly fell over. Having been drugged and on my back all day, the act of standing up and concentrating on the bowl resulted in my getting dizzy. Luckily, I was in the hospital, and my relatively minor injuries were immediately set upon by two interns, four nurses, and a janitor.

Eventually, they were done torturing me and let me go home, where I could both sleep and urinate whenever I wanted, a vast improvement over being in the hospital. Whatever they did, it worked, because now I no longer feel like I just ran a marathon while sitting in my easy chair. And hopefully no one else will need to stick anything in my heart for a really long time. I don't want anyone but you ladies messing with it any time soon.

Jake and His Explosives

A story about one of my closest friends, and one of the finest military officers I ever met. Boy, I do miss being stationed with him!

❦   ❦   ❦

First off, let me state that I love Jake dearly, and also that Jake is a very real man. Yes, I love a man. He is as genuine as they come, and his rough edges only make him that much more interesting.

Having said that, I can now say that he is one of *the* craziest sons-of-bitches I have ever met in my entire life. Every minute with him is an adventure, because I don't know 1) what he is going to say, 2) what voice he will use when he says it, 3) what exactly he is going to do, 4) whether or not explosives will be used and 5) whether or not we will end up in jail (usually as a result of number 4).

One of my favorite Jake stories involves beavers, a beaver dam, and, of course, high explosives. Jake bought a beautiful piece of property on 11 acres in pretty much the middle of nowhere, and built an absolutely amazing house on it. In that house, Jake co-habitated with his beautiful wife, and their beautiful baby. Outside the house, beavers co-habitated with other beavers, and built their own amazing (beaver) house, which we call a dam, on the property's creek. This would not have been a big deal, except that the aforementioned dam (as dams are prone to do) screwed up the drainage on Jake's property, resulting in a not too small lake behind Jake's house every time it rained for longer than ten minutes.

Now, most people would hire an exterminator to get rid of said beavers, but Jake is not most people. A smaller portion would exercise a little more violence and go beaver hunting with Dad's old .22 rifle. Jake isn't any of those people either. What people Jake *is* is a United States Marine Corps Combat Engineer Officer, and those guys don't do anything that doesn't involve explosives. *Lots* of explosives. As such, Jake proceeded to wire the beaver dam with enough explosives that the beavers in the next county would know what happened. And then, when he pushed the proverbial button, Armageddon was visited upon the offending beavers, and drainage once again occurred unobstructed.

That wasn't his only run-in with wild life. Jake has played golf about three times his entire life, and on one occasion he actually hit a gopher with one of his shots. Now, again, most people would just let the poor dazed creature slump off into the woods. A heroic few would try to nurse it back to health, generally concerned with the creature's well being. Jake pulled out his ever-present knife and finished the job.

There's more. Jake and I were riding around the military base where we both worked, out on the back road where the traffic is about one car or less every hour. As we were driving, I was looking out of the window daydreaming. Suddenly the truck suddenly sped up and swerved. I looked out the window, and saw the reason for the evasive action; a flock of wild turkeys. But then I noticed that my companion had swerved *toward* the portly birds, not away. He missed, but quickly pulled over and was about to remedy the situation with a .357 that appeared seemingly out of nowhere.

I politely asked "Jake, what the Hell are you *doing*?"

To which he replied, "I'm getting dinner, dumbass," and bolted from the vehicle after the now scattering flock of turkeys. I was in hot pursuit, because hunting without a license on a military installation was something I did not want to be on the wrong side of, for several reasons. First, brig time looks bad on the record, and even if they did just fine us, I was already broke, and didn't want to continue the tradition. More importantly, I was scared for my life. Jake's wife had long since given up on hoping Jake would show common sense, and she counted on me to exercise enough common sense for both of us. The consequences for failure were too horrid to think about. There wasn't a thing Jake feared on Earth, except the beautiful Mrs. Jake, and the thought of her roasting both our turkeys flashed through my mind as I chased after my pistol-wielding friend. I caught him just before he was about to send the biggest bird to the great beyond, and was able to convince him that no bird was worth the wrath of the mighty Mrs. He relented, and we walked back to the truck, him cursing the whole way.

I have mentioned that Jake is a Marine and a combat engineer. As such, no social event is complete without explosives and massive amounts of fire.

Therefore, Jake's annual January bonfire is a truly monumental event. He collects wood from his property for about two weeks, and starts the fire with a gallon of gasoline and a quarter stick of dynamite (left over from the beaver incident, I'm sure). Incidentally, this is the same way he starts the barbecue grill. Then we proceed to drink beer, eat grotesque amounts of barbecued meat, and burn everything we can find, including our eyebrows, usually. Late in the evening, after everyone has been drinking, there is singing. Sometimes, after that, there is gunfire. But everyone has a great time, at least as far as they can remember.

"Unique" doesn't even begin to describe Jake. He can be crude, rude, obnoxious, and mean, especially before his first cup of coffee. But, he is incredibly loyal, a complete patriot, and absolutely devoted to his family, his troops, and the Marine Corps. If I ever have to go into the trenches, he's at the top of the list of guys I want to go with.

And if he's carrying explosives, whatever happens will *definitely* be worth watching ...

How Not to Snowboard

A painfully true story about my first snowboarding experience. I plan on trying it again, as soon as I heal up.

❦　　　❦　　　❦

Compared to our ancestors, we have it pretty easy. We live in a fairly safe world. We have eliminated many diseases and have learned to take better care of ourselves. Thanks to OSHA and a general safety craze, we can go anywhere we like secure in the knowledge that thousands of safety dollars have been spent to prevent us from tripping and falling more than six inches. It's a far cry from when our caveman forefathers had to look both ways when exiting the cave to avoid being stomped by a diplodocus.

This kinder, safer environment has not come without cost. Because living a normal life is no longer fraught with adrenaline rushes, thrill-seekers have developed several ways to risk death, and pay for the privilege to boot. Sky-diving, hang-gliding, swimming with sharks, and any number of extreme sports are all testaments to how much trouble otherwise sane people go through in order to tease Mother Nature and the laws of physics. And, recognizing my own limitations and mortality, I have bravely steered clear of virtually all these pastimes. Until recently.

Not long ago, I had the opportunity to experience snow boarding for the first time. A friend of mine graciously loaned me his *very* expensive condo at a "local" resort (we will get to that later), and in order to experience something different I accepted. I was confident that my athletic ability would serve me well enough that I could at least pick up the gist by mid afternoon. My goal was to be on the double black diamond slopes by noon the following day.

And here begineth the lesson. First, very rarely is skiing "local," especially when you live in southern California as I do. For those of you that don't travel much, snow flakes are rare here, and without a few million of them lying around skiing is pretty dull. Because the snow wasn't coming to us, we had to travel to where the snow lived. So my friend Krista and I packed up and headed north, anxious to throw ourselves upon the snow and the slopes.

Because I had invited her, Krista graciously volunteered to drive, so I equally as graciously volunteered to pay for gas. This proved to be quite a financial burden on my part. Krista, though petite, does not conform to any stereotypes about petite women and "chick" cars. Krista drives a Ford Expedition, which apparently has 24 cylinders and gets 4 miles to the gallon. With a few well armed Marines riding in the back, Krista and her Expedition could easily conquer small European countries. Nevertheless, after a six hour trip down mostly a two lane road with no street lights, we arrived at the resort. And we only made four pit stops along the way—all of them because of me; Krista, despite her small size, has a bladder the size of Lake Erie.

Because we arrived late on a Friday evening, and since hurtling down a snow covered slope is best accomplished in daylight, we elected to meet up with some friends in a local tavern. The plan was to have a few social cocktails, after which we would retire so that we could get up early the next morning and begin our winter adventure. Instead, we embarked on a drinking binge reminiscent of ancient mariners returning to port after months at sea. We consumed mass quantities of beer and also several shots of something called "liquid cocaine." As a result, I fell down three times and I hadn't even seen snow yet.

The next morning came too quickly. I awoke at about 8 AM, and immediately began experiencing a hangover for which there was no equal anywhere in the world. Krista was surprisingly chipper (because she is Superwoman) and felt no ill effects from the mass alcohol consumption of the previous evening. On the other hand, Brett, a friend of ours who crashed on the couch, did not wake up at all. His hangover apparently dwarfed mine in comparison.

So Krista and I went for breakfast, and also to explore the resort town while waiting for Brett to regain consciousness. Krista told me that ski towns have a spirit all their own, and I was going to learn how right she was. We first stopped off in sporting goods shop to check on the late season deals. I used to think that I had a problem with fashion, until I saw what some skiers wear. I kid you not, one outfit was a furry, sequined brown vest, topped out with a purple knit hat with the head of a dinosaur on it. It was being worn by the proprietor, and it was actually one of the more tame things he had on display. I tried to buy it for Krista, but they didn't have her size.

From the sporting good store we went to the video store, intent on renting some sort of ski flick to put us in the mood while we resuscitated Brett. Actually, I was intent on renting "Totally Natural Teens" but Krista persuaded me via an elbow to my ribs that such things were not in my best interests. As we entered the store, we noticed the manager, and it was immediately obvious that people in ski resort towns don't marry outside the family often. "Simian" only begins to describe this kid. What was worse, he had a 1970's white-man afro-perm thing going, which he had failed to comb in two weeks. He didn't say much, just sort of walked around in circles behind the counter, but was helpful enough when we checked out. We left in a hurry before he drooled.

We obtained breakfast without further incident, and in a charitable act brought Brett back some coffee. We placed it near his head on the coffee table, and awaited the results. The smell wafted beneath the sheets, the pile of sheets and blankets stirred, and a shaking claw-like hand came out from underneath. It grabbed the coffee instinctively, and then retracted back beneath the sheets, placing the coffee next to the cheek of the still unconscious Brett. Alcohol had reduced this man from a confident, walking, talking human to a barely alive lump that actually cuddled with coffee.

Eventually, we were ready to go skiing. Except I wasn't going skiing, I was going snow boarding. The mathematician in me felt this would be a better idea, because skiing involved two boots, two skis, two bindings, and two poles, which adds up to eight things to go wrong. Snowboarding is one board, two bindings, and two boots, which works out to be three less variables, which I therefore figured *must* be safer. Such logical thinking contributed in a large part to my failing math earlier in life.

Unfortunately, I missed the lesson that I had planned to take because of our late start. No worries, Brett was a very good skier and snowboarder (when he wasn't unconscious), and Krista had been on skis since she was two. They would teach me and take care of me, and I would be black-diamond ready by the next day.

Well, they *tried* to teach me. Brett said, "don't worry, just something-something-something about ankles and toes and knees and look where you are going without looking where you are going and for Heaven's sake don't *ever* look at your feet." None of this made sense to me, but with the same instructions Krista got up there and went down the slope like she was born on the board. So, not wanting to look like an idiot, I proceeded to get on the board.

And then I proceeded to go down the slope like I was born on a merry go round.

I went around and around and *around.* I didn't see where I was going, couldn't see where I had been, and had even less of an idea about how to get between the two. At one point I was totally balanced and in control, heading down the slope, albeit completely backwards. Two seconds after that, I distinctly remember looking UP and seeing both my feet and the snowboard. When I finally hit the ground again, I immediately applied my "butt brake" and sat down on the slope. Careening to a halt, I realized that most of this chaos had occurred within fifty feet of where I got off of the chair lift, and I still had a good 400 yards of slope to survive.

The day did not improve. I kept giving it the old college try, and kept colliding with everything within a two mile radius. Trees, pylons, snow banks, other boarders, and in one unfortunate incident that I don't ever want to repeat, an elk. I was perhaps the most ungraceful, uncoordinated, untalented boarder to ever stink up the slopes in the southwest portion of this great country. Some of my wipe-outs were so spectacular that small children would applaud as they zoomed by.

After five runs down the slope which can better be described as "uncontrolled skids on my face," I had enough and retired to our lodge both to heal and to drink. The next day, as we actually were able to get on the slope *before* noon, I signed up for a lesson in hopes of avoiding the embarrassment of the day before as well as the potential for broken bones.

I met my group at the top of the "kiddy hill." There were five other neophytes as well as myself, all bent on mastering how to get from point A to point B without killing themselves or anyone in the vicinity. We were an interesting lot. Besides myself, there were two amputees, a guy in a wheelchair, an eighty-year-old woman, and a four-year-old. My ego was about to take another hit. Ten minutes into the class they were all doing *much* better than me.

The instructor was a snow nymph from Syracuse who strapped on her first snowboard about 33 seconds after she was born. She was very pleasant, and only made fun of my total lack of skill when she thought I couldn't hear her. In no time at all, she had the rest of the class balancing, turning, stopping, and doing one minor half-pipe trick. All except for me; I was falling, crashing, out of control, and only able to perform any sort of trick by accident. Convinced that everyone was progressing nicely but me, she decided it was time to get on the lift and go up to the top of the mountain.

For those of you that have never been on a ski lift, I will briefly describe the experience. It was like being chased across ice by my living room couch while a large piece of plywood was strapped to my feet. When the couch finally caught me, it grabbed me and immediately lifted me up 50 feet over trees, snow, ice, and skiers while it carried me to the top of the run. Once there, it spit me out like unwanted lima beans. I came to a halt after twenty feet of rolling, sliding, skidding, and cursing.

Upon being regurgitated, I found myself at the top of the same run that had bested me so many times the day before. With great trepidation, I approached the starting point with my classmates. One by one, we all began our journeys down the slope, hoping against hope that at least some of us would survive long enough to make it to the lodge below. Soon, it was my turn. I whispered a quick prayer, made sure I had plenty of curses and expletives handy, and started down.

And I was *great*. I was "on edge!" I was cutting and turning and swerving and at one point jumped clear over two of my classmates who had messily collided with a blind skier (who was way better than any of us were anyway). I was *the man* as I hurtled down the slope like I was *born* on this board. Of course, I had absolutely no control over any of this, and was screaming like a scared sissy *girl* the whole way, but when I finally came to a halt at the bottom, I had the admiration of my classmates and was completely non-dead to boot.

My spirits buoyed by this performance I raced to the ski lift to try again. Despite being once again regurgitated by the lift at the top, I nevertheless hit the slope for another run, anxious to build upon my previous success. Intently, I started my run, bound and determined to repeat my earlier feats. Instead, I went off the edge of the slope and into a tree. But, once I regained consciousness, I vowed that I would not be beaten, and pulled myself erect once more.

Most of the afternoon proceeded in this fashion. It was an epic conflict. Me winning small victories (not being thrown violently off the lift, actually staying on the slope, staying alive) but losing the war of attrition (twisted knee, torn jacket, minor head trauma). In the end, we called a truce. I agreed to stop trying to board, and the mountain agreed to stop trying to kill me. As an added bonus, I stopped bleeding all over the white snow. Both parties were happy.

I retired to the lodge, awaiting my companions, who had spent most of the day on triple black diamond slopes normally skied only by Norwegians trying to commit suicide. They had a blast, and were none the worse for the effort. We all retired to the condo to pack out, vowing to come back as soon as we could trick our benefactor into again giving up his place for the weekend.

I learned many interesting things that weekend:

1. Packed snow is *very* hard, especially when impacted at Mach 2.3.

2. Krista has a large bladder.

3. Liquid Cocaine is evil.

Note that none of these lessons were actually "how to snow board." But that's irrelevant, because I experienced the sheer exhilaration of the sport, and can honestly say I caught the snow boarding bug. I can't wait to get out there next season and try it again, eager to match my wits and body with the mountain. Krista is planning on coming too, if she's not invading Sweden with her Expedition that weekend.

Sleepwalking is Bad

One of those "truth inspires fiction" stories ...

❈   ❈   ❈

I have never been much for rules, but there are a few that I do think are important. "Never say bad things about the boss when he can hear you," is one. "Don't have sex with two different people who might know each other and can compare notes," is another. The most important one of all, though, the one that I try to live by every day, my credo, if you will, is the following: "Wake up in the same place you went to sleep." My thought is, if you wake up in the same place you went to sleep, you are in good shape.

Now, you would think that this would not be a difficult rule to live by. You would think that it would be really easy to actually go to bed in one place, and when you wake up, still be there. Now, I know there are some of you who are saying, in your geeky, nasal tone, "What about if you fall asleep on an airplane over North Dakota, and wake up over New England?" To that I respond, in a mature, sophisticated manner, "Jump, you geek, that's not what I'm talking about!" The point I am trying to make is that if you go to sleep in your bed, you should wake up in your bed, or at the very least, on the floor. You should not, for example, wake up in the frozen food case at the local supermarket.

I make this point because it appears that I have taken up a new hobby; sleepwalking. I don't know why I have decided to do this. It is not like I needed a new hobby. Being ignored by women and collecting beer bottles from around the world has kept me plenty busy, believe me.

The trouble all started about six months ago. One night, after I had one more last one at the local watering hole, I came home and went to bed, in my bed, in my bedroom, in my bed clothes. I awoke the next morning, on my couch, in my living room, wearing my underwear inside out. Even with all my artistic talent, I could not begin to imagine how this happened.

Since then, I have had increasingly more disturbing sleepwalking incidents. I have woken up in the bathtub wearing a bathing suit. I have woken up on the kitchen counter, perhaps preparing for the next evening, when I woke up on the dining room table, wearing nothing but the table cloth. I have woken up on the patio. I have woken up on the *neighbor's* patio.

I have tried several things to arrest my newfound desire to roam while asleep. I tried tying myself to the bed, only to wake up tied to the bumper of my truck. I have tried locking myself in my room, only to wake up locked outside of my house. I have tried sleeping with my boss's daughter, but that's a completely separate incident.

As none of my attempts appeared to work, I decided to submit to counseling. I made the appointment for first thing in the morning, but couldn't go because upon waking on day of said appointment I found myself at center ice of the local hockey rink, wearing a dress and fuzzy slippers. The doctor still charged me $120 as a "cancellation fee," and then told me I would require six straight weeks of therapy, running me about $500 a day, in order to cure my problem.

Always the economist, I have found a cheaper option. I have employed the services of one Mistress Elaine, who chains me to my bed for $65 a night. When I try and get up, she berates me and then proceeds to apply discipline with her riding crop. The arrangement is both cheaper and more rewarding than therapy.

If you want to hear more about this, I'm happy to talk about it. Just make an appointment with me. But please make it in the afternoon. It's a long walk from the frozen food aisle of the supermarket ...

Oh, How Cute. A Bear

The second story inspired by the "other" girlfriend, the one who grew artichokes as a hobby. This was the beginning of the end ...

❦   ❦   ❦

I'm pretty sure my new girlfriend tried to kill me last weekend.

Now, those of you that know me, and the unfortunate few who may have dated me may not be surprised by this. But she hasn't known me for more than a few months. Normally, women have to know me almost a whole year before they try to kill me.

I was out there visiting her in the great state of Washington (motto, "No, the *other* Washington.") and she decided that because it was a beautiful day and we were unlikely to get bitten by any sort of bugs or wild creatures indoors, we should go on a hike. I quickly agreed, so as to avoid having a romantic weekend by myself (I have had enough of those) and she promptly began to plan.

She had bought this "amazing" book about 100 hikes to do in Washington (no, still the *other* Washington) and immediately picked one that looked interesting to her, meaning it was far away and had lots of flowers. And so off we went. On the way, we stopped for a hearty breakfast at a local greasy spoon. We paid $8.99 to split approximately one-half of a pig. Our breakfast had sausage, bacon, thick bacon, Canadian bacon, biscuits with bacon gravy, ham, three eggs, and toast. Not only were we going hiking, but each of us was going to carry around an extra five pounds, just for fun. Well fortified (and feeling incredibly slothful) we got back in the car and drove to the trailhead. We got lost on the way, primarily because I was in a food coma and therefore neglecting my navigator duties. But we eventually found it and unpacked our gear.

"Gear" is probably too generous a term, at least as it applies to me. She was rather well prepared, with a backpack, water bottles, hiking boots, a sweat rag, emergency rations, a whistle, a compass, a flashlight, and the Declaration of Independence. Please keep in mind that I did not list "amazing hiking book." That will become extremely relevant later.

In contrast, I had a ball cap, two flip-flops (both left footed), half a can of soda, two sticks of gum, and some string. I also had a brand new shiny Leatherman® multi-tool, which I had twice been able to open, and once even without drawing blood. As we entered the trail, I read the trail report, posted at the trailhead by our friendly neighborhood trail ranger, Ranger Mike. It said some pretty innocuous stuff, and I wasn't all that concerned until I got to the last line. "Bear at Fisher Lake," it read. This caught my attention only because Fisher Lake happened to be exactly where we were headed.

My girlfriend, who had much more hiking experience than I did (she had been on two before) didn't bat an eye, so I assumed all was right with the world. After all, she was genuinely afraid of spiders, and therefore I thought that she would not set FOOT in a forest if there was a realistic chance of seeing something as big as a bear, which are much bigger than spiders. Besides, she really doesn't like bears, as evidenced by her constant abuse of my teddy bear Oscar. Suffice to say she acted as if it were safe, so I thought it was safe, so into the forest we went. According to my honey bunny, the trek was about six and a half miles, and would take us about 90 minutes. We would frolic at the lake, maybe get to grope each other a little bit, and then skip happily 90 minutes back out.

We began our journey in earnest, she to experience nature, me to finish as soon as possible so I could get back to watching football. The first part of the trip was actually pretty pleasant. It was cool, the bugs were reasonably non-aggressive, and the views were actually breathtaking. Enjoying Mother Nature at her best, I quickly forgot all about the bugs, the bear, my bookie, and anything else that was bothering me, and was whistling a happy tune as we enjoyed quality time together.

Until something rustled in the brush about 100 yards off. "Rustled" is probably the wrong word, as the small trees at the edge of the clearing we had just entered practically toppled over.

"Honey, did you see that?" I politely asked my snuggle monkey.

"See what? You're paranoid. C'mon, there are some flowers over here you haven't sniffed yet …"

And that settled *that* argument. We continued to advance into the clearing, and I checked my watch. It had been just about 90 minutes, so if she read the book right and I read my watch right, we should be standing in, or very near, Fisher Lake. Now, I will admit that I am no great woodsman, but even I could say with a fair amount of authority that there was no lake anywhere *near* our location. It was at this point that I politely suggested that my huggy wuggy take a look at the book, just to confirm that we were where we were supposed to be, since the lake was obviously not.

Well, things went downhill from there. She realized that she had forgotten the book, and then blamed me for forgetting to remind her (??). She assured me that the lake had to be here *somewhere*, and we immediately began searching for it by climbing up the steepest hill we could find, despite my insistence that water is normally at the *bottom* of a hill. This plan went from bold to tiring to exhausting to just plain *stupid* in a matter of minutes, and we stopped to reassess our options. Deciding that we really didn't *need* to see the lake that day, we began to retrace our steps, and once again approached the clearing where a half hour before I was accused of being paranoid.

As we arrived once again in the clearing, I immediately began scanning for whatever had "rustled" by us earlier in our journey. She immediately began sniffing flowers. As we worked our way across the clearing, we crossed a fairly soggy, muddy patch of earth, just right for making tracks in. Just out of curiosity, I studied the mud to see if we could determine what other creatures had been there recently. There were quite a few tracks made by other humans, but one set caught my eye in particular, probably because it had three inch fingernails. Immediately ruling out a poorly groomed hippy, as Ranger Mike would have warned us of such things, I could only surmise that the bear "at Fisher Lake" was actually taking a little hike of his own. On the bright side, at least we were close to the lake.

I drew a quick breath and immediately whispered to get my girlfriend's attention, so I could show her what I had discovered. She took one look at the tracks and promptly pronounced "Oh honey, you're being paranoid again. That's a dog."

If we had actually been married, I probably would have filed for divorce right there. A dog? Did she not *see* the *size* of the print there before us in the mud? If that belonged to a dog, then he was eight feet tall at the shoulder. I was just about to make a quite profound argument when across the clearing (which, incidentally, was where we needed to go in order to end this escapade) there came some more rustling. And look! This time, it was accompanied by a bear.

Not a teddy bear. Not a koala bear. Not any kind of cute, cuddly, I-wanna-hug-you bear. This was a real live, *real big*, black bear.

Now, I've been in situations where I have been a little scared before. I'm in the military, and it happens. The military life wouldn't be any fun if we only got to play in safe neighborhoods. But in those situations, I was armed and I was with other similarly trained, similarly armed people. So I didn't panic, but merely listened to my instincts, which told me to lock, load, and call in an air strike.

Unfortunately, I had nothing to lock or load, and there was no way to call the Air Force on my cell phone. It was Saturday, and they wouldn't have been working anyway. So after telling my instincts to pound sand, I admit I was a little scared and a little confused as to what exactly my next step should be. I was pretty sure that it should not be towards the bear, however.

My girlfriend, anxious to help, immediately began offering sage advice which she "remembered" from her reading of hiking books.

"Find a stick to wave at him!" she said.

Heck, sounded good to me! Now, I had been tripping over sticks throughout this little jaunt all morning, but of course now as I searched the immediate area, there was not a single stick to be found. Desperate, I whipped out my trusty Leatherman, opened the toothed saw attachment, drew blood, and immediately began cutting down the nearest small tree. If the bear was not aware of our location prior to that point, this announced our presence in resounding fashion.

In addition to my frantic cutting, we also began singing a tune. I don't really remember much of it (I was sawing *very* intently) but it did have the words "no bears" in it quite a lot. So picture in your mind two college educated adults in a meadow singing "no bears, no bears" while one of them frantically worked to cut down a small tree while being watched by a bear who was probably doing his best to avoid dying of laughter. That should give you a good visual of the situation.

I finally got the tree down, and we immediately began working around the clearing, me dragging the tree, in order to get back to the trail on the other side, all the while hoping we could get back to the car without seeing what the insides of our new friend Mr. Bear looked like. While dragging the tree, I was at the same time whittling it into what I hoped would be a spear, but which in reality would probably only serve as a toothpick for Mr. Bear if he got that close.

It was a pretty tense situation, although you wouldn't know it, from the cheery "no bears" song we were singing. Eventually the bear got bored and just loped off. We regained the trail and loped off ourselves, though at a slightly faster clip. After about twenty minutes, my heart rate subsided, and I was reasonably sure we might survive the ordeal. We were headed back to the car, we hadn't been eaten yet, and so I was feeling better with every step. My companion quipped that the pace seemed "a whole lot faster" then when we were marching in, but I had enough of nature for that particular Saturday morning and was trying to cover ground as fast as possible in order to end this ordeal.

On our way back, we began passing other hikers headed in the opposite direction and, I was convinced, certain doom. Some were couples, some groups of three or four. Invariably, they all asked some inane question, just to be friendly, like, "How's it going?" or, "Having a good hike?" My girlfriend, never short on words, used this as an invitation to launch into a play-by-play accounting of our hike to this point, especially our bear encounter, complete with her brilliant tree-waving idea. The onlookers listened in rapt fascination as she described how we saw a bear, and only by her quick thinking were we not eaten alive, because I was paralyzed by fear through the entire encounter. I don't really remember it that way, but she's been known to take a few creative liberties.

I lost count of how many groups she relayed this story to as we extracted ourselves from the forest. I know I got a little upset when she began using her cell phone to call people about the whole thing, and I about lost it when she ran out of friends to call and just began dialing random numbers. "Hello. Guess what? *We saw a bear!*"

When we got back to the car, we immediately recovered the amazing hike book to try and find out why two educated people had such a hard time finding a fairly sizable lake. We soon found that she had only *slightly* misread the book. The lake was nine miles away, not six. And in an opposite direction. And in another county ...

But that was water under the proverbial bridge, and besides, she was cute, so having survived the adventure we packed up and headed out. As we were driving back to her place, I began to leaf through the front of the book, trying to find the "How to Deal With Bears" section. When I did, I was amazed at what I learned.

"Rule number one for dealing with bears: If the trail report says there are bears in the area, *go somewhere else*." Hmmm. Well, we certainly blew that one. I kept reading.

"Rule number two: When spotted by a bear, *do not* make any threatening moves, such as waving anything in his general direction." Oh, like maybe a small tree, perhaps? Hmmm again. Good info to have.

I immediately pointed out to my lovely companion that her recollection on the matter of bear encounters was less than perfect. She accused me of being paranoid, and stated that my personal hygiene was less than perfect. Then she made me buy her dinner.

Next time, I'm taking my chances with the bear.

What the Hell is a "Moosefoot?"

My friends had some more choice names for me after reading this one.

🍁   🍁   🍁

My given name isn't really all that exciting, or funny for that matter. If you think about it, most people's given names aren't that funny—Frank Zappa's kids aside. So I admit that I am absolutely proud to be part of a culture that must award a nickname to just about anyone, either for a valid reason, or just as well for one that doesn't make any sense at all.

If you think I'm kidding, think of any man you have ever met with the last name "Murphy." I'll give you $20 if he has never been called "Murph." I know three Murphy's, and they were *all* called Murph. *Very* confusing when more than one of them was in the same room. We had to start numbering them. Almost as common is the moniker "Smitty" for someone with the last name Smith. Finally, anyone with a long last name starting with the letter "Z" is almost guaranteed to be known by that letter at least through high school.

Reflecting on my own life, I realize that I have had several nicknames. My dad used to call me "Tiger" when I was young, though I have no idea why. It was miles ahead of the nicknames given to my younger sister and brother, which were "Boopie" and "Moosefoot" respectively. More on that later.

College saw me referred to by virtually my entire class as "Balls," a play on my last name. The third week of our plebe summer at the Naval Academy, I was dubbed "Balls" by one of my classmates, the immortal Harry Boynton III (who was NOT called "Tre"). Sometime later he even gave me a hat from a local bar of the same name, which I wore every day until we graduated, and still own. Most of my classmates did not even know my first name. The week before graduation, while walking with my parents, I passed two of my female classmates. Both of them said, "Hey Balls," as a friendly greeting, which confounded my mom and frankly impressed my dad. To this day some of my college friends *still* refer to me as Balls, which in light of my medical history is pretty damn funny.

Back to Moosefoot. When my younger brother was about four years old, he received slippers for Christmas. These were no ordinary slippers, though. These slippers each looked like the head of a moose; sort of like Bullwinkle, but not really. He wore them everywhere. I think it was my father who began calling him "Moosefoot," but *who* started it doesn't matter. What does matter is that the name stuck, and stuck hard. Not only did we almost forget my brother's given name, but "Moosefoot" became a word in my house that had more meanings than a sideways glance from a hot woman. It could be at any given time a term of endearment ("I love you, you Moosefoot."), a term of derision ("you stupid *Moosefoot*,"), a deity ("in the name of Moosefoot,"), an adjective ("all moosefooted up,"), and an expletive ("oh, *Moosefoot*,"). Keep in mind that my family is fairly educated, and reasonably capable of expressing themselves without resorting to made-up words. Nevertheless, Moosefoot entered our vocabulary and has remained there to this day. Recently, my sister and I were having an argument, and as her final, decisive statement, my 27-year-old badass Army Captain whoo-yah warrior sister closed with "You, you, you ... *Moosefoot!*"

And it didn't stop there. I met and fell in love with a young woman who I wanted to introduce to my loved ones. Because we didn't realize she was evil, she was soon accepted into the family, and we felt we no longer had to hide our idiosyncrasies and general craziness from her. She picked up on the whole Moosefoot thing, and then *she* started using it regularly, and it morphed into our term of endearment for each other (in both its original form or the slightly more tender "Moosie."). Again, the fact that we were supposedly educated people didn't stop us at all.

Fast forward ten years. I'm still educated, but older. Because the evil one was out of my life, I met another wonderful sweet woman (who for the record was *not* evil).

We got along quite well, and of course there comes a huge first in every relationship, a time which neither party ever would or could forget. Of course I am talking about the first time I saw my new significant other without her socks on.

Now, I do not have a foot fetish. Actually, I am sort of anti-foot, and if it wasn't for getting around would have no need for them. But I am also anti-dirt, and therefore wanted this creature to relax comfortably on my couch without getting it dirty, which required her taking off her shoes and socks. Because she was very much pro-couch, she did this. And then I saw *them*.

Apparently, God had gifted this young creature with the most unique toes I had ever seen. They were long. And when I say long, I mean *loooooong*. If she ever became a *Playboy* centerfold, her toes would show up on the back cover. *That long*. Now I'm caring, and oh so sensitive, so far be it from me to call attention to any sort of physical abnormality. But I could not pass this up. I tried, I really did, but somewhere the words escaped my mouth, "Good God, woman, you have *Monkey Toes*." And so a new chapter in the nickname saga was written. Though not as widely used as Moosefoot was, it nevertheless became our interchangeable nickname for each other. This developed new problems, because we both addressed and signed our e-mails Monkey Toes, and so it became difficult to tell who was writing whom.

There have been other variations on the monkey theme, each used to denote a different woman. "Cuddle monkey" was one, and "Monkey pants" another. I don't even know what the heck "Monkey pants" means, but I am fairly easy to amuse, and anything preceded with the word "monkey" is going to get a smile out of me.

My girlfriends have had nicknames for me too, but as most of them are unprintable and horribly damaging to my ego, we will have to avoid that discussion.

Ok, What Did I Do This Time?

I can't tell you how often this has come up. It's already happened a few more times since I wrote this.

❦　　　❦　　　❦

Any man my age is used to being on the receiving end of female ire. I look back at my thirty plus years with a sense of wonder regarding the various and creative ways I have managed to upset so many different women. Whether it be for stuff I did, stuff I didn't do, stuff they thought I did, stuff I took, or pets I stuffed, the list is unique, long, and not without involvement from local authorities.

All of the wrath generated by the actions above I graciously accept, because I took part in bringing it about. I am a man, and a slave to my hormones, and also hideously bad at dealing with women anyway. I therefore deserve pretty much everything thrown at me for the heinous acts committed and noted above. However, it is important to realize that I am only accepting responsibility for sins *actually committed by me*. Acts committed by me *in a dream* do *not* count, and frankly, I'm tired of being blamed for them.

Yes, I know it sounds stupid, and some of you may be sitting there saying "that's preposterous." Well, you are right, it is preposterous, but it's happened, and it's happened enough that as soon as a woman tells me she had a dream my first question is "OK, what did I do *now?*"

Usually, I'll be sitting at home some morning, enjoying a soda and some educational TV like Bugs Bunny while clad in only my boxer shorts and a smile. Suddenly the phone will ring and one very disturbed female will be on the other end. The conversation starts with my saying "hello," and then holding the phone back six inches from my ear as a barrage of profanity flies out of it.

"You monkey-hugging cork-stopping (many expletives deleted) how could you do that to me?" she says, loud enough to be heard by my neighbors, despite the fact that they may be vacationing in Japan.

At this point in the discussion, whatever woman "I" have managed to upset begins to chronologically list in excruciating detail whatever *her* subconscious made "me" do in her dream. I have, in the course of some of these ladies' dreams, committed murder, committed assault, and committed unnatural acts with their pets. I have left them at the altar, left them at the mall, left them at the movies, left them at the store, and left them in a walk-in freezer. I have slept with their sisters, their mothers, their best friends, and their high school science teacher. I have stolen, raped, burned, pillaged, and generally made myself more of a nuisance than most Viking tribes. And twice I was gay.

And those are just the pseudo-realistic complaints. Never mind the time I caught grief for having an extra set of hands, or the time I took my arm off and gave it to her, or the one time I possessed super powers but accidentally dropped her while flying over Manhattan.

Now, everyone knows that guys hate to apologize, even when caught redhanded with one hand in the cookie jar and the other on a virgin's knee. Really, the only thing worse than being forced to apologize for something you did is being forced to apologize for something you not only didn't do but didn't even really happen.

Nevertheless, that's what I'm expected to do, time after time, because these women had too much dessert or too much to drink or watched a scary movie or whatever before hitting the rack. And when those ill-made decisions result in nightmarish consequences, apparently it's easier to call me up and demand an apology than it is to realize that *they* had the dream, and are in the end *way* more responsible for the fact that I impregnated their hair stylist than I am.

So, ladies, I propose a truce. I won't hold you responsible when you and your cheerleader gymnast friends turn me down in my dreams if you stop holding me responsible for going to Las Vegas when we are scheduled to be married in Cleveland. Deal?

Thou Shalt Not Miss Wing Night

I attribute this story to some very close friends. I don't miss much about college, but I do miss them.

🍁   🍁   🍁

Everyone has a favorite tradition from college. Whether it be running naked at the first sign of snow (those would be the geniuses at Princeton) or flinging yourself into the nearest body of water after your last parade (that's a favorite from the Naval Academy), college traditions abound. But there are also those personal traditions from college that we create for ourselves. The traditions and the friends we create them with help us get through what is for many of us the most challenging four years of our then young lives.

My friends and I were no different in this respect, and we centered our tradition on two very key college elements: beer and chicken wings. Every Wednesday night of our senior year, we would starve ourselves all day in anticipation of that holiest of holies, Wing Night. The wing-and-beer special at our favorite bar started at 10 PM, and we were in our seats by 9:57, salivating with anticipation. It was a really classy place, with a floor, ceiling, and even walls, so we felt like we were really stepping out for the evening. As an added benefit, it was only a ten minute walk (and 25 minute drunken stumble) from our dorm, and that was a big deal, because we were on a pretty tight schedule. Because we weren't very bright, we were at a military academy, and as such had to be in our rooms defending our beds from the forces of communism by midnight. Therefore, we had a *lot* of beer drinking and chicken wing eating to cram into a fairly short two hour period. We attacked this problem and the wings with zeal.

There were three of us that formed the core of the group. Besides myself, there was Mike "the Hammer" and Noel "the Unlucky." Noel was so named because he was subjected to so many of my attempts to hook him up with women that normally would appear on reality shows involving plastic surgery. We also had several cameo appearances by Noel's future wife, called Amy the Liver, as well as Kimi the Short, Diamond Dan, Hot Dog Man, and Dino.

Dino was there almost enough to qualify as a regular. He actually really enjoyed coming out with us, but Noel, Mike and I were engineers, and Dino was an English major. Since the bar was dimly lit, he could risk being seen with us, but didn't want to take too many chances of being labeled a geek-lover. He usually only participated twice a month. Hot Dog Man has a real name, but none of us remember what it is. We invited him out for Wing Night once because he was a pretty funny guy, and he came along, speaking boldly about the many chicken wings he would consume. At the last minute he ordered a hot dog instead. The barrage of comments, insults, and bleu cheese that this generated boggles the mind, but it was so memorable that we invited him back on several more occasions just so we could repeat the experience.

As any great ritualistic society might, we had rules. You were only excused from the group if you had two tests the next day, but even that was considered a somewhat weak excuse. If you only had one exam the next day, you damn well better be in your chair come game time. At one point both my esteemed colleagues gave me a ration of you-know-what because I was seriously considering not attending wing night due to a serious stomach flu. I gave in to their taunts, and did my best to keep up. I don't know much about medicine in general, but I can say from experience and with reasonable accuracy that chicken wings and beer are not anywhere on the list of things you should be eating when you have the stomach flu. I was vomiting more than a supermodel after an all-you-can-eat buffet.

The social pressures aside, the event itself was truly a glorious experience. The wings were brought out basted in Tabasco sauce, and were hot enough to melt paint off the walls. Likewise, the beer was cold, plentiful, and best of all, cheap. We ate and drank and told stories and made fun of each other and generally just reveled in the camaraderie of the moment.

The beers that were on special were 32 marvelous ounces. Most of us drank two during each outing. However, there were a few true overachievers that went above and beyond and pushed things to the next level. One night, as the rest of us looked on with awe, Noel and Amy consumed *three* 32 ounce beers in the two hours allotted. We immortalized this occasion by printing our very own tee-shirts, emblazoned with a hastily drawn coat-of-arms for our little group, and dubbing us "the 96 ounce club." The names of our club members were proudly printed on the back of the shirts, and we become celebrities, if only in our own minds.

Even the end of the evening provided entertainment, as if you have never seen seven or eight very drunk people try to divide up a check, it's pretty entertaining. If three of them are engineers, you have missed a very amusing spectacle indeed. The Hammer often tried to make things easier by counting on his fingers and toes. We went through this *every* week, despite the fact that wings, two beers, and tip *always* worked out to be $10 per person.

The ritual didn't end with the bar tab, though, at least not for all of us. A stickler for tradition, Noel insisted that he would only do his navigation homework *after* returning from our wing night debauchery. This was indeed a bold move, as navigation is a pretty important subject at the *Naval* Academy. The outcome usually provided the most comic of results, especially towards the end of the semester, when his navigation problems became more difficult. At one point, while plotting the most efficient course from point A to point B, he was able to cut *hours* off the times proposed by his other classmates. This was because he plotted his course over a peninsula. Another time, he proposed anchoring his ship in Cleveland. As it turns out, he was simply training for his naval career, when on several occasions he was forced to navigate while drunk.

And he wasn't the only one who committed his share of foibles after wing night. One "morning after" there was a desperate panic among the group when we couldn't find Dino. He had come back with us, pretty inebriated but still functioning, and was checked in on the rolls by the watch in time for lights out. But the next morning he was no where to be found. Searches were organized, and one of the searchers was female. While searching the dorm where Dino lived (on a *different* floor from where Dino lived) she felt nature calling and ducked into the female rest room. And then she tripped on something. Specifically, she tripped on Dino. Thus ended perhaps the greatest manhunt ever spawned by chicken wings.

Despite our wing night episodes, and several other equally non-academic practices, we eventually graduated. Noel headed to the west coast, Hammer to the Marine Corps, and myself to Florida for flight training. Dino missed associating with geeks so much he went to nuclear power school and then to the submarine community. We are lucky if we see each other once a year, and luckier still if we are all together in the vicinity of that bar. Whenever we are together, and wherever we are, we always re-enact our wing night ritual, complete with the drinking, the camaraderie, and the arguing over the check. The only difference is Noel doesn't have to do his navigation homework afterwards.

I Love My Truck. Oh, and My Girlfriend, Too

I know this is going to get me in trouble, but I can't help it!

🍁　　　🍁　　　🍁

Recently I was having a discussion with the newest woman in my life. I was just getting ready to call her my girlfriend, actually, when she opened her mouth and tragedy struck. I was telling her how much I *love* my truck, and by love I mean that emotion that only a man can feel for a thing of beauty like his very own personal four-by-four. And as I was almost finished with this emotional, tear-jerking outpouring of sentiment, she looked at me and said, "Y'know, it's just a truck."

That was it, she was done. Out the door. Obviously I have no future with a woman who cannot understand that sacred bond between man and machine, that emotion that can only be based on total trust and devotion.

I realize I sound like a nut, but I am convinced that my truck is the only woman in my life that will ever truly understand me. And fully aware that I am trespassing on so many "cucumbers are better than men" lists, I will nevertheless list the reasons why I feel that way.

1. **Trucks do not talk back.** You could call it nasty names (only in a fit of passion, mind you. You wouldn't actually *mean* any of them), insult it's lineage, or just vent on it, and it will take it all without batting a visor. In contrast, most women I date begin the backtalk even before I finish speaking.

2. **Trucks can be turned on with a key.** No super-expensive gasoline at a fancy service station, no sweet nothings you don't really mean. Turn the key, she's ready to go. Anytime day or night. In contrast, women require everything to be just right. And then they may actually consider thinking about being turned on.

3. **Trucks can be turned *off* with a key.** When you have reached your final destination, you turn the truck off, and it sits there quietly waiting for you to return so it may follow your next command. I won't bother contrasting that feature with a female. Nothing even comes close.

4. **Trucks always look good, even dirty.** You could take your truck out in the mud, roll it over a few times, and drive it through a pig sty just for good measure, and it will *still* be beautiful. Try *that* with a woman.

5. **Trucks don't care how we look.** I could go over to my truck wearing my worst jeans, having not shaved for three weeks, and smelling like a wet dog, and my truck will *still* be turned on (when I turn the key, of course. See above.).

6. **Trucks require gasoline, oil, washing, grease, filters, vacuuming, tune-ups, fluids, belts, hoses, air in the tires, hundreds of dollars in maintenance, and a host of other things.** In comparison, human women are ridiculously high maintenance.

7. **Trucks let you drive other trucks.** You could drive your truck to a lot full of *hundreds* of other trucks, and then get inside *every one*, and your truck will still happily drive you home afterwards. She'll even take you to dinner on the way.

8. **Trucks don't make you ask for directions.** Trucks are happy just being with you, and don't really care where you are going as long as you, the driver, are happy. They don't even care if we get there late.

9. **Trucks go exactly where you want them to go.** Hit the gas, turn the wheel, and it goes exactly where you tell it to.

10. **A truck full of gas is a good thing.** Enough said on *that*.

11. **Trucks can be traded in for a faster, newer, flashier model.** And you don't have to give your old truck half your stuff to get rid of it, either.

12. **Trucks don't need cuddling.** You can abuse it, be as dirty as you like with it, and generally do anything you want to it. And you don't have to hold it, caress it, call it the next morning or even acknowledge its existence afterwards.

13. **Trucks come with a warranty.** Ever try to take a woman back to her parents because she was defective? Trust me, it's not easy.

There you have it guys, thirteen reasons why trucks are better than women. I proudly showed this list to my future ex-girlfriend, hoping it would help her understand why four wheels and a tailgate mean so much to me. She just smiled that "you're not getting any" smile all women learn in high school, and handed me her own list. "Top fifteen reasons why you're an idiot …"

I'm Not Worthy

Just about every word of this is true. Probably in my best interest to avoid this woman (even if she is out of jail) but it has made for some serious bragging rights.

❧   ❧   ❧

Despite some of the horrors I've relayed earlier, dating can be a lot of fun, and I know when I *finally* convince some young lady to go out with me, I do the best I can to make sure she enjoys the evening. Holding open the door, telling her she looks nice, and helping her with her chair are all standard fare. Dressing appropriately after a shower where one partakes of both soap *and* a towel is also a necessary ingredient to a fun-filled evening.

Just as important as manners and hygiene is where one actually *takes* his date. For instance, all the manners and soap in the world won't get you anywhere if your idea of "dinner and a show" is 7-11 for hot dogs followed by watching kids skateboard in the alley.

It sounds like this is leading up to my describing the absolute best date I ever took someone on. That would be foolish, as I am single and if I do that I will be setting up a pretty tough standard for me to live up to in the future. So instead, I will tell you about the most memorable date someone ever took *me* on.

Now, before we get started, I would like to point out that while I am macho, manly, and basically a stud, I see no problem with a guy being asked out by a girl, especially if the guy is me and the girl is cute. And that's what happened here.

We will call her Trudy, because I don't want her coming after me when she gets out of jail. We met in a most romantic style, via the personal ads in the Washington Post, where the personal ads are actually *more* accurate than the articles. We went out a few times, and as happens when young, hormone-driven people consume too much alcohol, ended up having a sleep-over at her house one Wednesday night. Now possibly my performance was over and above what was expected of a male of my age and experience. More likely, she had horrendously low standards. But either way, the next afternoon, I got a phone call at work.

"Hey, it's me," she said.

"Hello, you," I replied, trying to place the voice.

"Listen, in view of your performance last night, I wanted to get on your calendar for Friday, before someone else does." Apparently, she thought my reputation was slightly better known than its actual "non-existent."

"Um, OK. What do you want to do?" Knowing full well that I didn't care *what* we did, as long as I got a shot at an encore.

"Just be at your house, dressed nicely, at 6 PM tomorrow," she said, and then hung up.

Being in the military, I was used to taking orders, and was appropriately cleaned, shaven, and dressed as 6 PM rolled around the following night.

My phone rang, and a gentleman by the name of Mort told me that he was downstairs, ready to pick me up. Trudy had sent a car for me. This was a new one on me, but because I was young and had never been kidnapped, I went along with it.

The car was glorious. It was a Lincoln town car, complete with uniformed driver in the front and today's paper in the back. He whisked me to my lovely's place of employment without saying a single word to me. Upon arrival, my date for the evening immediately took me to an intimate little bar, where she paid for two rounds *and* rubbed her leg up and down my thigh. At the time, because I wasn't making much money, I wasn't sure which I appreciated more.

Following drinks, we drove. And drove. And drove. And we ended up in what I can only describe as the middle of nowhere, at a little restaurant that I swear was built in someone's basement. On a painted board was an Italian name that had more vowels than any name I had ever seen, be it Italian, Indian, or Hawaiian. When we went inside, my date told the maitre'd "Luigi sent us, and said you would take care of us." That was apparently all he needed to hear, because we were immediately and with no further delay whisked to a private dining room.

Once seated, we were set upon by two waiters who almost killed each other trying to get to us first. They brought us a bottle of red wine, a bottle of white wine, a bottle of champagne, water, and an antipasto the size of lower Manhattan. Menus were nowhere to be seen.

The next course was a veal chop three inches thick which cut like butter. It was accompanied by some vegetables so exotic I couldn't recognize them, and some bread that was baked in the back room by a small Italian man imported solely for that purpose. As we feasted, I was beginning to wonder how I was going to pay for even *half* the tab. But just as I would get really worried, they would shove some delicacy or another in front of me, and gluttony would take over.

When finally it was time for dessert, the waiter brought us the dessert tray. As I was pondering over which of the tempting offerings to choose from, the point became moot as the waiter simply left the entire tray and walked away. Despite being stuffed, I made a valiant effort and in doing so practically doubled my blood sugar.

And now, the moment I was dreading: the *check*. Only it never showed up. She said "C'mon, let's go," and we *left*. I thought for sure that Vinny and Guido in the back room were just waiting to gun me down for the dine-and-ditch, but we walked out without dropping one thin dime. And the maitre'd thanked us on the way out!

Well, she picked up the check, but there is no free lunch (or dinner, in this case). Perhaps I forgot to mention that Trudy had attended the University of Minnesota on a hockey scholarship. She was perhaps the strongest man, woman, or alien I had ever come across, and she was absolutely going to make me work off dinner.

This ends the "great date" part of the evening and begins the "someone please save me" portion. Sometimes a romantic evening is like a beautiful ballet performance. This wasn't one of those times. This evening was more like a championship hockey game, with all the bumps, bruises, and broken teeth that go with it. I have never been so physically intimidated or abused by the fairer species. I was definitely *not* leaving until she got what she wanted, and whatever I wanted was pretty much irrelevant to the proceedings.

I'm not sorry to say that our torrid relationship came to an end shortly thereafter. Surprisingly, I did nothing to end things, as the Federal Courts did it for me. The love of my week was indicted for embezzlement, and her jail time really put a strain on our relationship. She was awarded conjugal visits, but I looked at her sentence as a sign from God. Maybe someone both less criminally inclined and less likely to kill me was more my speed. I said my goodbyes (in an email) and promptly moved to a different state.

Beat that for a memorable date story. I dare you.

Fantasy Meets Reality, Porn-Style

This is about as risqué as I get. You could say that the underlying theme is that I finally realized what's fantasy and what's reality, but really I was just trying to write a story with "adult situations."

❀　　　❀　　　❀

I've come to a pretty important conclusion. As much as I would like it to be otherwise, I've got no choice at this point but to accept the fact that I've been lied to for years. Yes, the wool has been pulled most thoroughly over my eyes. I've been hoping and praying and wishing, but after all this time, it's finally dawned on me that life isn't at all like a porn movie.

I became suspicious a few months ago, when, after watching an X-rated marathon, I ordered a pizza to be delivered to my home. Imagine my surprise when the delivery person who arrived was no where near my age, incredibly unattractive, and oh by the way a guy. Deeply disturbed, and with my curiosity piqued, I began exhaustive field research. With the help of the local video store, I watched literally hundreds of adult rated films, spanning the disturbingly broad spectrum of human sexuality. Cheerleaders, midgets, nurses, slumber parties, midget-cheerleader-slumber parties, I took it all in, and took copious notes. At the same time, I began to compare what I was seeing to what I observed going on in society around me.

Psychologists from around the world will argue that it would be impossible to watch hundreds of adult movies without it having some negative impact on a person's psyche. I can't comment on that, because only recently have I stopped drooling and humming weird seventies porno theme music out loud

20 hours a day. But despite such impediments, I couldn't help but notice that my life was a *lot* more boring and a lot *less* filled with loosely-clad loosely-moral'd women.

My girlfriend provided the grounds for the initial observations of my research. First, she refused to engage in any sexual conduct in or on top of a moving vehicle, and further would not "give up the goods" in any sort of public place. Nor would she even entertain the idea of entertaining any of my friends, co-workers, or the local college football team. Finally, she became so frustrated with my research that she dumped me, and refused to have good-bye sex with me, my best friend, or both of us together. Nor did she run crying in a tight little negligee over to my good looking female neighbor's door, looking for female compassion.

Her behavior, plus the pizza disappointment, really caused alarm, and on top of that, many other incidents began to open my eyes. My slightly older but still very attractive neighbor asked me to come over and "unclog her drain", and she actually wanted me to *unclog her drain*. Not only that, but when I did, she simply said thank you and expected me to leave. She didn't even comment on the size of my tool! Later that week, my slightly younger but very amazingly attractive neighbor came by to borrow some sugar, and when I gave it to her (the sugar, I mean), she just said thank you and *left*. And as if that wasn't enough, it got worse.

I had a doctor's appointment, and only one of the nurses was even *close* to my age. And she was only moderately attractive. And she did not come in and try to give me any sort of exam before the doctor did. The doctor was a man, and when he asked me to drop my drawers, there was no group of eager, gorgeous young female medical students to watch the proceedings or perform embarrassing tests. Later that same day, the girl at the checkout counter made no attempt to pick me up, and when I got home there were no busloads of sorority girls broken down in front of my house. And when I went out later, I didn't see *one* girl in tight shorts that twisted her ankle roller-blading and needed to be helped back to my place.

The week continued, and when I went to the library for further research, the librarian was ugly and old. No older, lonely woman accosted me in the stacks, and no young co-ed grabbed the last copy of "Sexual Positions of the Orient" at the same time as I did. No bisexual foreign exchange students moved in upstairs, and at no time was I asked to participate in an exciting new study testing the latest human sexuality drug.

You would think that this would be enough overwhelming evidence. Certainly for the average guy. But we all know I'm not average; I'm *way* dumber than that, and I wasn't convinced. So I continued to search for more proof.

Finally, through sweet talk, respectful behavior, alcohol, and lying, I was able to convince a poor unfortunate female creature that she needed carnal knowledge of me in order to make her life complete. She had seen several X-rated videos, so I thought she could help me with my study. As we moved into my bedroom and frantically removed our clothing, she took one look at my naked form, especially that part of me south of the waist, and blurted out "Wow, life isn't like a porn flick, is it?"

A good looking girl laughing at my naked form. OK, *now* I was convinced …

Jibe Ho!

Another "Rob meets nature" story ...

❉ ❉ ❉

One of the many things that were mandatory in that prison where I spent my college years was learning to tie all kinds of nautical knots. Another was a really bad haircut. Neither of these was particularly amusing, and though scars from both are still present, they aren't worth boring people with. However, learning to sail was also mandatory, and it did provide a fair amount or entertainment both then and now, though not usually to me.

While we were in our first summer at the Naval Academy, we had to take a crash course in sailing and seamanship, and were taught how to sail all kinds of vessels. These "vessels" were small one-person boats called "Lasers," five-person boats called "knockabouts," and bigger boats called "yachts." Eventually, some of my classmates sailed on destroyers, but that was much later. For now, we would all begin our careers the same way. The "sailing" part for the majority of us consisted of learning how to take the boat off the pier, how to capsize it, right it, capsize it again, and put it back. Some of us were slightly more advanced in that they could make the boat go where they wanted it to go most of the time, but most of us just tried not to drown or be involved in any major collisions.

My roommate at the time (we will call him "Scott" because that was his name) succeeded in not drowning, but came up short in the "not being involved in major collisions" department. Scott had an unfortunate run-in with the Harbor Queen. The Harbor Queen was a touring ferry that held about 200 people, plus a bartender and a captain. Scott was in a Laser, which only held Scott. Luckily, Scott survived with only minor damage, although his Laser was not so lucky and was last seen headed to the bottom of the harbor.

During the course of our instruction, we learned that when sailing it helps to have wind. On our second Laser instruction day, the wind was noticeably absent. However, because the Navy had scheduled my platoon to sail that day, we were going to sail that day, even if it was snowing and the Bay was frozen and Martians were landing, because that is how things are done at the Naval Academy. So we all paddled out to the middle of the bay, tied ourselves together, set Scott out to watch for the Harbor Queen, and took a two hour nap on the water. For two hours that plebe summer, life was good ...

Despite the Academy's best efforts, I survived sailing, and obtained the qualifications they forced us to obtain in order not to get yelled at. I didn't even think about sailing again until over a year later. I was no longer a plebe at the academy, trod upon by all. Instead I was a sophomore, a "youngster" in the vernacular of the school, and therefore ignored by all. OK by me, as I was plenty tired of getting yelled at. Anyway, my high school girlfriend came to visit one day during my summer assignment at school, and she wanted to go sailing. As I wanted to raise *her* sails, I readily agreed, and immediately bribed my roommate into coming with us, because we needed two qualified people to handle a boat big enough to carry all of us.

We arrived at the pier, and immediately and proudly presented our qualification cards to the sailing master, who snickered and then signed out a boat to us, no doubt hoping we would be lost at sea. The day was bright, the water was smooth, and the wind was pleasant, so we, armed with our seven hours (each) of sailing experience, were anxious to hit the water.

Things went smoothly for the first hour. We tacked and jibed and the buoy we were using for reference was comfortably in the distance. Then the wind died. Just *died*. We were dead in the water, in irons, whatever else you want to call it, we were *not* moving. I had no idea what to do, and no idea how we were going to get back. At least the buoy was still in the distance, so I didn't have to worry about damaging the boat.

Later that afternoon, the sailing master sent his flunkie out to remind us that we had to have the boat back in an hour. Relieved to see someone who actually knew and cared where we were (or at least where the boat was), I thought quickly and immediately began showing one of the international signs for distress by waving my arms over my head. The flunky waved back, and *turned around*. Now we were really screwed.

It was at this point that we began debating who was going to jump in the water and tow us back to shore. Because I had gotten us into this mess, the votes were heavily in my favor. However, my girlfriend had been swimming since she was about three, and I figured that the best chance of survival lay in getting *her* to tow us in. The debate grew more and more heated, and so distracted us that I lost situational awareness, and we slammed into the buoy we had been so hoping to avoid. In doing so, we also scared the hell out of a family of pelicans who made their home on said buoy. This was not the glorious career on the high seas that I had imagined when I joined the Navy.

It was apparently at that point that the sailing master realized that the only way he was ever going to get his boat back would be if he sent someone to rescue us, and we were ingloriously towed back to the sailing center, arriving two hours later than planned. We were safe and on dry land, but I was so embarrassed and annoyed that I decided not to sail again for a while.

That "for a while" turned out to be about twelve years. Fast forward to just a few months ago. My friend Ron decided to take up sailing. This in itself was pretty funny, because he was stationed in Yuma, Arizona, where there isn't a body of water bigger than a swimming pool for miles. About two weeks after he passed his qualification test, he asked me if I would go sailing with him, because the boat required one brain but two sets of hands to operate. I agreed, and we had a pretty good time sailing around San Diego. Sailing seemed to have gotten easier in the 12 years I had been hiding from it. We completed the voyage without throwing up, tipping over, or sinking, and had a great time in the process.

So when he asked me to go again, I readily agreed and we enjoyed another beautiful sailing day on the San Diego bay. This second experience was only slightly marred by the fact that Ron tried to pitch me overboard with a sharp swing of the tiller while I was precariously perched on the bow. I am used to such things from him, however, and we had a good laugh about it.

For our next adventure, we both decided that we should bring some female companionship. We figured that in a small boat in the middle of the bay, they would have no choice but to talk to us. He brought this lovely girl Polly, whom he adored and was one day hoping to marry, or at least have a relationship that lasted longer than the evening news. I brought Sally, who was mildly attractive, somewhat fun to be around, and, we would soon find out, incredibly prone to sea sickness. I should have known we were in for a rough day when as she boarded the boat she asked, "Is it too late to ask for Dramamine?"

Too late to turn around, we boldly pushed on. Within 200 yards of the pier, the wind kicked up and blew Sally's hat off her head into the water. We were all a little surprised by this, except maybe Sally, who pulled another hat immediately from her bag and didn't even blink. Apparently, she lost hats all the time.

Ron decided that because we had gone along the calm, easy-to-navigate south bay on our first two excursions, perhaps we should "kick it up a notch" and go towards the north bay. The north bay was windier, choppier, and inhabited by sharks. This deterred Ron not in the least, and we proceeded north.

Things went well for about the next twenty minutes. It was windy, and a little choppy, but not oppressively so, and we began to relax and enjoy the moment on the high seas. Soon, however, things took a turn for the worse. As we got farther from shore, the high seas got higher, the motion of the boat became more pronounced, and Sally became progressively greener. Soon she was sitting down. Then she was lying down. Then she was lying down with her eyes closed. Then she was lying down with her eyes closed and mumbling something that sounded like a prayer for death. Finally, she mustered up enough strength to put her head over the side and, in the ancient tradition of the sea, to feed the fish with her breakfast. Apparently, she was quite ill and had eaten a *large* breakfast, because she went on feeding the fish for quite some time.

When she had finished hurling everything out of her stomach, she relaxed and felt better. We could now turn our attention completely to avoiding the ship that was bearing down on us. We were all so enthralled with watching Sally vomit that we forgot silly little things like situational awareness and seamanship. We narrowly missed getting run over by a container ship from Japan (which though smaller, more efficient, and cheaper than container ships built here, was still pretty damn big).

The excitement passed, and we decided that we could better enjoy the high seas from the comforts of our living rooms, so we decided to head back. Just as we began to come about, though, a gust of wind slammed into the sail and pretty much rocked us all the way over to starboard. I was on the high side of the boat, looking down at a terrified Sally, whom was desperately trying to grab my extended hand in order to prevent going into the water. The water came over the starboard side, and we all thought we were going to tip. Our fearless Captain Ron sort of just froze in the moment, and we all waited for the inevitable dunking. Then, miraculously and *ever* so slowly, the boat righted itself, and soon we were all celebrating the fact that we were reasonably dry and still afloat. Ron smiled, Polly hugged him, I high-fived Ron, and the celebrations continued. Sally decided to celebrate by throwing up again. This time, because we were all such good friends after surviving our near death experience, she didn't even decide to hang her head over the side, and instead just let go with a mighty stream immediately into the wind, which promptly blew back all over Ron. As you could imagine, he was less than pleased.

We made best speed back to the dock, returning several hours earlier than expected. We had had enough. We were all a little wet and a little seasick. Sally was minus her breakfast plus one hat, and Ron was wearing much of the contents of Sally's stomach. We agreed that it had been a full day.

Sally apologized profusely over the huge lunch I bought her to satisfy her now raging appetite. We weren't at the "hold me when I vomit" stage of the relationship yet, so we haven't seen much of each other since. Ron went back to Yuma, Arizona, where the sailboat population is about zero. I am into my second 12 year hiatus from sailing, and am pretty happy about it, because on land there are fewer incidents of projectile vomiting and significantly less chance of getting hit by a ferryboat. I do plan on continuing my naval career, provided I can do it on dry land most of the time.

Every Naval Officer Needs His Teddy Bear

This story is the first "official" mention of my fiancé. No more girlfriend stories for me!

❦   ❦   ❦

Stuffed animals have always been prominent in the history of my family. Since I was little, I can remember that my younger sister had a virtual menagerie of stuffed dogs, cats, bears, monkeys, and at one point, a bull. She referred to these as her "kids," and the pick of the litter was a Snoopy-lookalike named "Jack." Jack was a Christmas gift, and may have been her favorite out of pity, seeing how she ripped off his nose that first Christmas day. My father's favorite activity while my sister was young was to stick various members of her "family" in the freezer, thus ensuring that she would one day need serious therapy.

When my brother was born a few years later, he began his own collection. Because, at age two, he did not have much financial power, he did this by stealing. He took my sister's second favorite animal (behind Jack), a stuffed dog appropriately named "Doggy" as his own. From this humble beginning, his collection grew, and he soon had several others creatures, including a green dragon named "Boobala," a stuffed worm complete in a Swedish mountain-climber's outfit, and a seven foot white gorilla named "George." All of these he took turns either hugging or having brutal wrestling matches with, which is pretty much the same way I treated my brother. One of our (my) favorite traditions was "worm beatings." This involved me pummeling my brother with the worm, which made a pretty decent weapon when used against a three-year-old.

My father, having grown tired of his freezer antics, developed new ways to torture us as the years progressed. One day, my brother was on the front lawn picking up sticks, a chore we did constantly in order to "build character." Unbeknownst to him, my father was upstairs, stalking his prey. As my brother diligently picked up sticks, he would occasionally hear noises overhead or behind him, like something large and soft and furry flying through the air and then landing somewhere around him. My brother caught on about the time Dad launched his eighth stuffed animal (a polar bear named Pokey) out the second story window at a scale speed of about Mach seven. My brother watched as Pokey traveled in a parabolic arc through the sky, to land with a dull thud about 20 feet from him, amidst several other stuffed animal carcasses. He immediately began screaming at the top of his lungs for my dad to stop this needless abuse. My father responded by increasing his rate of fire from one animal every 30 seconds to eight per minute. My brother came as close to a coronary as any six-year-old ever has.

Noticeably absent from all these stories is yours truly. I only had one stuffed animal growing up, a skinny monkey named "Billy." Billy got his name because on his t-shirt in bold letters the word "Billy" was spelled out. He was supposed to have a cute tuft of white hair on his head, but he was an economy stuffed animal, so it thinned rather quickly. As a result, a few months after I got him he just looked like he had mange.

Like most children, I did eventually establish strong ties to a stuffed animal. Unlike most children, I was twenty-two at the time. One day upon arriving home from work I saw a rather large teddy bear sitting in the hallway outside my apartment. He was sporting a sign which said, "Free to a good home." I immediately snatched up both him and the sign and entered my apartment to share my treasure with my two roommates. One was asleep, so I immediately placed the sign on him and showed my new-found lifelong companion to my other roommate. She decided on the spot that he should be named "Oscar." And Oscar has been with me ever since. I never leave him behind. He has driven across this country with me twice, riding shotgun and receiving waves from small children nationwide. He has even deployed to Spain with me. (He enjoyed it, but was happy to return to the states.) Oscar is my buddy, and I personally think every professional naval officer should deploy with his stuffed teddy bear.

For a long time things were pretty stable. I had a few other stuffed animals, but mostly they were cutesy gifts given or received from one or another woman

I was trying to impress. Recently, however, there has been a veritable population explosion, so I have divided the horde into the Varsity and Junior Varsity.

The JV sits on the bed in the guest room. They are a bunch of stuffed animals whose origins or names for the most part I can't remember (with a few exceptions: Garfield and Elmo are both gifts from my parents, but they have hard plastic pieces so they don't get to go on my bed with the Varsity.). They are the first line of defense when my friends bring small children over that need to be kept occupied.

The Varsity is lead by Oscar, and his younger brother, a bear named Timmy. Timmy was the "son" of my fiancé, and used to wear an Oakland A's jersey all the time, but they traded her favorite player, so now he is usually naked unless he gets into the laundry again. Then there are the twin monkeys, Mike and Charley. They don't look anything alike, except for being monkeys, but they wear matching US Naval Academy Football jerseys, which in a former life were beer coozies I received at my ten year reunion. They are usually in the company of Patty, who is also a monkey, and the sole female in the group. She is tiny and pink, but can often be seen riding around on her brothers' necks inciting them into more mischief. And finally, the newest addition to our family, a pink pig appropriately named "Stinky Pete."

We (mostly me, I think my fiancé just goes along to keep me happy) refer to the Varsity as our "children." When going on trips, one of the smaller ones always accompanies us. It is important that stuffed animals broaden their travel horizons at every opportunity. We also practice parenting skills on them, lecturing them when they get into mischief, or lecturing each other when we commit some parental faux paus. These usually include picking up a child by its face or else using it as a projectile to interrupt the other one's studying (that's mostly me again, actually). We refer to the later as "flying monkey attacks" even if we happen to grab an actual non-monkey.

While our current clan does provide entertainment, we have started thinking about getting a dog. The main drawback as I see it is that I am pretty sure the dog would eat his less-animate brothers and sisters, and I for one am not ready to promote cannibalism. When I tried to mention this to my fiancé, she threw a monkey at me, so I will have to table the discussion for a later time.

Thank You Note to My Family

This piece can't even begin to cover all the things for which I am grateful to my family. I started writing this when I was away from my family during the holidays for the first time, but have added to it since. Feel free to use any of this with your own family.

❦   ❦   ❦

OK, I realized I haven't lived that long. I am only 32, and if all goes well, I probably will live at least another fifty years. Longer, if I marry someone I don't like. Still, there have been an incredible amount of good things that have happened to me, or that I have received, and most of those have been largely due to my family. I couldn't possibly begin to thank my folks and the rest of my family for everything they have done, but I can at least hit some of the highlights. Some of these may sound a little weird, but remember, this is written for a more narrow audience than most of my other stuff. Here goes …

First, Mom and Dad. I have been very blessed when it comes to parents. My folks aren't heroes, and they aren't legends, and they probably aren't perfect, but they are two of my closest friends in this world, and most of who I am and what I have accomplished I owe to them. So, Mom and Dad, thank you. Specifically, thank you for the following, in no particular order except that which they occurred to me:

> For buying me Christmas presents when I was so young I wouldn't remember where they came from and couldn't even say thank you properly, unless drooling on your shoe counts as a thank you.

> For hugging me whenever I needed a hug.

For wiping my nose, or changing my diaper, or changing my sheets after an "accident," and all that other yucky parent stuff that you never got thanked for.

For letting me believe in Santa Claus for as long as you did.

For my sister and brother (we will get to them later).

For taking so many pictures of me when I was young, and so many when I was young and naked, and for showing so many of those pictures of me young and naked to girls I was trying to impress by bringing them home to meet you.

For buying me lots of Lego toys, which, in addition to giving me something to leave all around the basement floor, stimulated my creative and design energies, fueling my desires to become an engineer.

For not hating me when, after being trusted with our family camera while on family vacation, I left it under a picnic table, allowing it to be stolen along with all our pictures.

For buying me the Aeronautical Lab Kit, which though you never really saw me play with it, is still one of the coolest presents I ever got.

For making me be nice to my sister until I woke up and realized that I *enjoy* being nice to my sister.

For braces.

For making me play basketball, and being so supportive, win or lose.

For leaving Aunt Maryanne's house on Thanksgiving day, just so I could get home and go to basketball try outs the next day and get cut for the third straight year.

For teaching me to catch a football thrown *right at my head* without breaking my fingers.

For buying us popcorn during the movie *E.T.*, even though you had said we could only have one thing, and we picked Twizzlers, and decided half way through the bag that we didn't like them.

For making my lunches every day before school, even when it was just baloney and mustard on white bread.

For sending me money every time I needed it, and lots of times when I didn't.

For coming to visit me at the Naval Academy.

For giving me such a wonderful home to return to anytime I want.

For reminding me that I could succeed at the Naval Academy, but that I did not *have* to succeed at the Naval Academy.

For welcoming Wendy and Tricia and Jill and others into our house like they were family, even though you didn't always like all of them.

For all those clothes you bought me that I never really appreciated while growing up.

For my first car.

For my second car.

For the help with my third car.

For coming to meet me at the airport in NJ when I was there between flights en route from CA to Baltimore. You drove 45 minutes one way to see me for ten.

For letting me go to most parties.

For NOT letting me go to some parties.

For giving me and my friends a ride home from Sandy's house in east nowhere on New Year's Eve when I had screwed up the plans so bad no one knew who was driving whom anywhere.

For talking to me about girls when I needed it, sex when I didn't, and the difference between sex and love when I got caught stealing one of Dad's *Playboy*'s.

For taking me to work with you when I could be of help.

For letting me ask Pam to go to the movies in eighth grade, even though we never actually went.

For flying down to be with me when I was in the hospital.

For putting up with me when I was recovering not so much from what cancer did to my body as from what it did to my head, which took a LOT longer.

For making me build the rock wall.

For going all out every Christmas, for no reason other than we were your kids, and despite our behavior you felt we deserved it.

For taking me to see the Yankees play.

For teaching me to cook.

For curfews.

For relaxing curfews.

For coming to the pistol range with me.

For sending me Christmas presents when I was deployed, just to make sure I didn't forget it was Christmas.

For understanding why I had to deploy in the first place.

For always looking surprised and grateful whenever I brought home a Christmas ornament or some other art-class creation from preschool or kindergarten or elementary school, even though it was very difficult to tell what it was even supposed to be, and for always acting like it was made of gold.

For my high school ring, that I cherished for two years, until I lost it.

For my college ring, that I will cherish forever.

For always keeping an eye on me, except when you knew it was best to look away.

For buying me a guitar, even though I have the musical talent of a mostly deaf duck.

For understanding why you have a 32-year-old son who loves the Muppet Movie, sleeps with a two foot teddy bear named Oscar, and occasionally barks for no reason.

For being there when I needed you, and giving me space when I didn't (or thought I didn't).

For holding me accountable for my actions.

For reminding me that I was special, even for no other reason than I was your son.

Wow, that's a lot. And I didn't even get it all. Truth is, I only scratched the surface, but I hope they get the point. I am not done yet, though. I still have some other thank-yous that I need to put out there. Up next is my sister. Now, I know I wasn't always the best big brother (though the part about me trying to sell her still can't be proven), and I know I didn't always tell her how important she was to me or how proud of her I was. And now that I realize what a dope I had been for a lot of the time, I am halfway around the world and can't tell her nearly as much as I should. But maybe this will help. To my sister, thank you:

For looking up to me when I didn't deserve to be looked up to.

For making me realize that there were times I was being very uptight for no real good reason

For making me music tapes and sending them to me.

For making me wait for you when I would drive you to school, because if I didn't I would have missed out on quality time with you, time that I sorely wish I had back.

For introducing me to all your cute friends in high school, college, and afterward.

For understanding why you have a 32-year-old brother who loves the Muppet Movie, sleeps with a two foot teddy bear named Oscar, and occasionally meows at you.

For meowing back.

For knocking down my block buildings when I was little, so I could rebuild them and make them better.

For racing around the basement with me, you using your doll stroller for a race car, and me using your toy shopping cart.

For answering all my medical questions with the knowledge of a very competent nurse and the compassion of a very loving sister.

For, despite my sometime less than positive influence at times, developing into a truly remarkable, attractive, intelligent, accomplished young woman of whom I am so proud that words fail me.

Again, I know I am leaving out a lot, but I hope she gets the idea. Now on to my brother. My "little" brother, who is ten years younger than me and has been taller than me since he was 13. He has grown up so fast that I can't even begin to fathom where all the time went. Yesterday I was dressing and undressing him, and throwing him around the room, and today he is taller than me and beating me regularly at arm wrestling. He does still need help getting dressed, though. To my younger brother Dan, whom I love dearly despite the fact that so often we don't seem to agree, thank you. Thank you:

For being my boxing partner.

For giving me someone to play strategy games with, someone who is every bit as good at them as I am, and someone who beats me on a regular basis.

For giving me another reason to go to high school football and basketball games.

For becoming a good driver.

For not becoming too angry with me when I talked down to you, or lectured you, or tried to hurt you, and realizing that in my own warped way I was only trying to help you.

For routinely beating me at most video games.

For always sounding happy to talk to me on the phone, no matter how near or far I was.

For not telling Mom about all the times we cooked hot lunches when we weren't supposed to.

For making me laugh by doing "piggy snorts" with your plastic cup.

For being such a good kid at heart.

For always getting me such good Christmas presents.

For being a younger brother that I can trust and teach and learn from. Unlike my relationships with the others, which have matured and probably won't change too much more, the relationship between you and I will become deeper and more meaningful the older we get. I am so looking forward to that.

Well, that about does it. Now there are lots of other people who have had profound influences on my life, and they all are worth mentioning, but not here. These pages are for my family, whom I love, cherish, and owe virtually everything to. I don't really know what made me write this, in this way, at this time. Maybe it is just a feeling that it is long overdue. Maybe it is because in the back of my mind I know that my profession as a military officer is more dangerous than many, and that I might not get the chance to say it. For whatever reason, I did it, and I'm glad.

The cool thing about my family is that I probably didn't have to.

978-0-595-36343-8
0-595-36343-1